MONAMAU
&
BOOKS OF AFRICA

IMAGINE THE AFRICAN FUTURE

Elli Glevey was born and raised in Ghana and educated in England. He studied mathematics and was awarded a doctorate in Philosophy of Education from the University of London. He taught mathematics for many years in schools and colleges in England and later worked as a mathematics educator at the University of London. His books include *Thinking & Education* and *On Being African.*

IMAGINE THE AFRICAN FUTURE

Elli Glevey

MONAMAU
&
BOOKS OF AFRICA

MONAMAU
&
BOOKS OF AFRICA

Published
By
Monamau Limited Jointly with Books of Africa Limited.

Monamau Limited,
Kemp House, 152 – 160 City Road, London EC1V 2NX. England.

Books of Africa Limited,
16 Overhill Road, East Dulwich, London SE22 0PH.
United Kingdom.
www.booksofafrica.com
admin@booksofafrica.com
sales@booksofafrica.com

ISBN: 978-0-9571458-1-8

Printed in England by Catford Print Centre, London, England.

... the ancestors are yet to return
with tales of the ravages of the lesser jihad.
The epistle of the bitter harvest
has long lost faith in its own demeaning charm.
A legacy pleading desperately
for resurrection to come to its overdue rescue.
The climate is steadily changing,
with the invigorating outline of tomorrow.
Morning light inscribes the true path
for the day to joyfully follow,
casting rainbows across
the dark southern skies in bold colours.
The long awaited purification
begins with the birth of green.
Behind stands Osiris completing the hollowed rites.
Now, fully transformed by pure exuberance,
Africa, it is time to return to hope.

from the poem Africa
by Elli Glevey

CONTENTS

PREFACE

About five years ago I was stunned by the projections reported in a statistical research report on African development that I read. The report propelled my initial exploration into various likely future scenarios for Africa, which provided the material for this book.

Knowing that there is nothing certain about envisaging the future did not prevent my effort to sketch one for Africa. However, its vastness and complexity contributed exceptional difficulties in doing so. My effort to overcome these difficulties led to my focusing on Ghana as a means to discussing Africa's future.

Ghana's independence in 1957 provided a good backdrop as it announced a new bright future packed with confidence for all Africans. How successful has Ghana been in leading the struggle for African development? What has been the response of the rest of Africa? These questions helped to shape a path that guided much of the ensuing considerations offered in the book.

It has been an exhilarating experience in the attempt to imagine the African future and hope that it provides a platform for positive discussions of Africa. Any errors of fact or interpretations are my own.

London, November 2017   Elli Glevey.

ACKNOWLEDGEMENTS

My gratitude to all the people who helped to shape the outcome of this book. The casual conversations that offered unexpected inspirations and opportunities for exploration are too many to count but not entirely forgotten.

However, it is important to mention those individuals who standout in providing the needed support critical for bringing this venture to fruition.

Moses Anafu for bringing his expertise as an African historian to provide very insightful ideas and helpful comments. Nigel Watt, for his exceptional editorial support. Will Glevey, for his dedication in offering the vital technical assistance for the production of the manuscript. And finally, to my family for their enduring support.

INTRODUCTION

The story of Africa and its people raises much contention with regard to their present station in the world and their possible future prospects. However, assuming our planet continues to exist far into the imaginable future then what will Africa look like in the next hundred years or two hundred years for example? How well will Africans be doing over this period? These questions are not trivial, as we have no means of correctly predicting the future without plentiful assumptions and guesswork. Irrespective of these limitations we human beings often attempt to conjure up various possibilities concerning our future and from time to time some visionaries come close to giving us sketches of our future that occasionally appear to take on some semblance of reality. Figures in the chronicles of mass African liberation movements such as Marcus Garvey and Kwame Nkrumah gave us vivid visions of possible African futures many decades ago that now appear to show some remarkable similarities to the African condition in our present time. Considering the progress made in Africa since the winds of independence swept across the continent over half a century ago what are the future prospects for Africa?

The future for Africa requires vigorous discussions in which Africans must take the initiative to generate possible scenarios and considerations of how best to meet the requirements that those scenarios present and the feasible solutions available. While there are no guarantees as to how the future might unfold and the results that it may entail, there are some benefits in doing so and the challenges involved should not provide any pretext for casting the exercise aside. As already indicated, to think about the future can widen our understanding of how our actions today impact on the events and outcomes of tomorrow. Let us for example consider population. Assuming the population forecasts that have so far been projected remain more or less unchanged into the foreseeable future, then Africa is very likely to become the most populated area on earth by the middle of the present century. Given this scenario what would it mean for city, town and country planners? What would be the implications for healthcare requirements? What sort of provisions should be made for education and training? Would there be any need for the encouragement of some sort of birth control? These are examples of some of the pertinent questions that need some exploratory answers at the very least as a prelude to deeper considerations of the issue.

In the attempt to discuss the African future the material presented in this book is divided into three parts each consisting of three chapters. The discussions in Part One focus on the progress of African states from decolonisation to the present time. In Chapter One a broad overview of the advancement made so far by some of the leading African states provides the focus for the discussion and in addition sets the scene for the discussions in this part of the book. Chapter Two highlights the relationship between the Western world and Africa and similarly, Chapter Three discusses the increasing influence of the Oriental world in Africa.

Having gained independence the responsibility now lies with Africans to create their own future world and that is the focus of the discussions in Part Two. Thus Chapter Four briefly examines current developments in Africa and some of the challenges facing Africans in their attempt to rise above the debilitating effects of domination for centuries. Chapter Five covers the unfolding environmental issues in the world and the possible consequences that they may have on Africa and its inhabitants in the foreseeable future. Some of the challenges facing Africa such as conflicts and the opportunities that their diversity as a people offer for their future will inform the main points for the discussion in Chapter Six.

The aim of the discussions in Part Three is to use the preceding considerations of Africa's progress so far to discuss some possibilities concerning its future prospects. The crossroads at which Africa finds itself at this juncture in history and the choices it must make provide the main focus of discussion for Chapter Seven, these choices however, require Africans to take responsibility for the path they decide to follow and Chapter Eight examines the arguments for doing so. In Chapter Nine a view of the African future and some of the key elements for wellbeing and prosperity form the main topic of discussion. Finally, some closing remarks outlining a conclusion to a topic that essentially has no conclusion mark the termination point for our discussions concerning the African future.

PART ONE

IN OUR TIME

The demand for independence in Africa brought with it the intoxicating early years of freedom that held promises of better times ahead. However, decades later these promises remain to be fully realised. How far have Africans progressed through the last century to the present?

CHAPTER ONE

BEARING WITNESS

A careful consideration of the African experience throughout the twentieth century can highlight the difficulties that Africans have endured at home and in the Diaspora. This period witnessed the successful struggles for independence across the African continent (and for some significant civil rights in some parts of the Diaspora particularly for those in the Western world). However, soon after having won their freedom Africans quickly became embroiled in the crossfire of the ideological warfare between the two super-powers of the era namely, the now defunct Union of Soviet Socialist Republics (USSR) leading the communist nations, and the United States of America (USA) leading the capitalist nations. The Cold War as it became known plunged Africa into a devastating arena of proxy wars for decades, resulting in unimaginable suffering and degradation of Africans.

The struggle by African states to seek their own form of government after gaining political independence and in some cases during the fight for independence provided the perfect condition for proxy wars in which the USSR and the USA often got involved by supporting opposite sides in various conflicts. Such polarizations were clearly manifested in Angola when Cuban forces and equipment from USSR were deployed in Angola to impede USA backed apartheid South African intervention when the Portuguese in 1975 withdrew after the Angolan War of Independence.

Both the USA and the USSR considered the Angolan conflict crucial to the global balance of power and to the outcome of the Cold War (and gaining access to natural resources played a major role). To this end, both powers and their allies invested significant capital and effort into creating a proxy war between the two power blocs. Ultimately, the Angolan Civil War became one of the longest and bloodiest of the armed conflicts during the Cold War.

The destructive impact of the Cold War in Africa from its beginnings in the anti-colonial nationalist politics to its horrendous final stages in the killing fields of Congo, Rwanda, Liberia and Sierra Leone to name a few, is enshrined in the distortions of the continent's material and human development.

The dissolution of the USSR in the latter half of the twentieth century, which contributed to the ending of the Cold War, has not yet resulted in any substantial improvement in Africa as its inhabitants face a long and dangerous journey toward the establishment of some form of political, social and economic stability and development. This journey is particularly perilous as intermittent violent conflicts in parts of the continent fail to find permanent peaceful solutions. These conflicts, which continue to be fuelled by so many factors including poverty, greed, corruption, perceived ethnic differences and in some cases religious intolerances, provide the background for the on-going weaknesses of institutions vital to the promotion of peace, wellbeing and general development of communities.

A question that is to be honestly answered by Africans is this: After more than half a century of self-determination in many parts of Africa and elsewhere in the Diaspora what are the future prospects? As a source for some tentative answers let us very briefly examine the progress that some of these African states have so far made.

True Confessions

The growing evidence in support of Africa being the cradle of human evolution over thousands of years (Wells, 2003) could lead one to draw favourable conclusions about the immense contribution of Africans to the foundations and durability of the progress that we human beings have so far made. However, the present state of the African world easily raises questions such as: 'if Africans gave the world its first civilization then why is their present progress so harshly stunted?' Let us consider a few specific examples.

Ethiopia

This part of East Africa containing a vast highland complex of mountains from where much of the River Nile flows out through Sudan and Egypt before emptying into the Mediterranean Sea is the symbol of African independence from Antiquity to the present. Ruled under a long tradition of monarchy, Ethiopia is one of the very few places in Africa that did not totally fall under prolonged foreign colonial rule. However, for a brief period in the mid 1930's Ethiopia was invaded by

Italy for a number of fashionable reasons including the desire to assert its power and acquire resources for the Italian economy at the time.

The short-lived Italian occupation of Ethiopia from 1935 to 1941 among other things contributed fresh insight into the deep-seated and painful crisis concerning African identity. The attachment of Africans to Ethiopia is rooted in their consideration of Ethiopia as a model of African liberation due to its ancient history and independence; consequently, the Italian invasion precipitated overwhelming outrage throughout the African community. Africans in the Diaspora as well as in other parts of the African continent were willing to volunteer their services to defeat the Italians. Some managed to find their way to the battlefront while others contributed by other means such as petitioning European colonial governments, writing propaganda materials, and raising funds, however meagre, for the war effort.

However, the attention on Ethiopia brought to light some of the complexities existing within the Ethiopian culture regarding racial identity. Emperor Haile Selassie in an interview on his arrival in London when he fled from Ethiopia affirmed that Ethiopians were not, and did not regard themselves as Negroes as they were a Hemito-Semetic people (Sbacchi,1997). This remark added some validity to the allegations at the time that Ethiopians considered themselves superior to Africans and viewed dark skinned people of African descent as inferior and identified them by the use of the term 'shankalla', which can be understood as 'slave.' A number of possible explanations for Haile Selassie's statement may include firstly, his need not to be identified with the African due to the derogatory implication that it entailed as a consequence of slavery and the perceived debased character of the African. Secondly, his need to present the Ethiopian case to the European powers at the time demanded dissociation from the perceptions of African inferiority.

In his frustration, Marcus Garvey, the well known diasporan African Nationalist leader criticised Haile Selassie on various issues including his racial disloyalty, his failure to educate the Ethiopian people, his failure in not speeding up the eradication of slavery in Ethiopia, and above all, for being a coward by fleeing Ethiopia and deserting his people in their hour of need. In spite of the racial identity controversy Africans considered Ethiopians as essentially of African origin and continued to campaign for their liberation. During the Second World War African soldiers from Ghana, Nigeria, Kenya, South Africa as part of the British and Commonwealth forces in East Africa as well as French West African soldiers contributed to the defeat of the Italians in Ethiopia. After the war and the return of Haile Selassie to Ethiopia he remained relatively isolated from African affairs as he disagreed with the radical aspects of Pan-Africanism and consequently was reserved in his support for the growing agitation for African liberation from colonial domination.

The ambivalence of the Ethiopian attitude towards Africa and its policy of isolation gradually changed and finally, in 1963 Haile Selassie publicly recognised the contributions made by Africans in the Diaspora and on the continent to help free Ethiopia from the Fascist occupation. After the major struggles for independence by African states the Ethiopian capital was chosen by the newly independent African states as the site for the headquarters of the Organisation of African Unity (now known as the African Union), a gesture that marks Ethiopia not only as belonging to Africa but as the leading spiritual foundation for African progress. In 1974 Haile Selassie was deposed by a band of his military officers based on their accusations of corruption and incompetence of his government and on his character and performance as a despot, thus bringing to an end the oldest Christian monarchy in the world (Tibedu, 1995). The military takeover led to the death of thousands of Ethiopians as the junta sought to transform an empire riveted to deeply rooted traditions (stretching back to antiquity) into a modern socialist state that respected all its citizens as equal. This project failed after a few years as the nation descended into one of the bloodiest civil wars on the African continent. Thus far, how do we account for Ethiopia's implicit role as the foundation and model for African progress? What kind of leadership role has it advanced for taking Africa through the twenty-first century and beyond? The extent to which this role has been fulfilled will be left for future generations to examine.

Liberia

In contrast to Ethiopia, the area in West Africa called Liberia came into being as a consequence of the Atlantic slave trade. With the support of The American Colonization Society in the early 1820's emancipated slaves from America were transported to this West African region. Liberia was (in all aspects) the American solution to the 'Negro problem' as the real goal was to purge America of Negroes. Over the next two decades the community in effect became an American colonial outpost with American Colonization Society employing agents to govern the colony. In 1847 the legislature of

Liberia declared it an independent state with the last appointed governor elected as its first President. Liberian society developed into three groups consisting of the settlers with African American lineage; liberated slaves from slave ships embarked for the Caribbean and finally the indigenous native people.

The Americo-Liberians[1] and their descendants dominated the life and politics of Liberia for the first 133 years after independence. The progress of the Americo-Liberians in their new environment incorporated segregation and severe victimization of the native people they came to meet. The absurdity of this unfortunate turn of events is that the Americo-Liberians came to reproduce some of the negative behaviour and degrading conditions that characterised the situation of the African slaves in the Americas from which, they were attempting to escape. In an interesting personal account of life in Liberia Dennis (2008) chronicles how the enduring destructive effects of slavery and racism impacted on the formation of Liberian society:

> Instead of a pluralistic or integrated society, there were two Liberias – two social and cultural realms that didn't mesh. Presidential rule was the only thing that integrated Americo-Liberians and natives/African-Liberians. During the 1930's and 40s, when the Americo-Liberians said "United we stand, divided we fall," they meant their own unity, not national unity. Their insecurity kept them from seeing the national interest as their own best interest (p51).

The failure of Americo-Liberian rule was inevitable as cultural racism prevented social unity, which resulted in the exclusion of the vast majority of the Liberian population. A towering personality in Liberian politics was William Tubman, who ruled from 1944 until his

---

[1] This group consists mainly of African American settlers

death in a London clinic in 1971. Tubman was a controversial figure who was admired and hated in equal measure. While Liberia had the image of a Western democracy, in reality Tubman who made all decisions and consolidated the Americo-Liberian privilege epitomize 'one-person' rule.

William Tolbert who became Tubman's successor initiated some liberal reforms including the creation of an opposition party thus returning the country to a two party system after a century. Tolbert's reforms led to criticisms and the unleashing of some of the deep underlying forces that drove the economic and social disparities between the Americo-Liberians, who had dominated the country since independence, and the various indigenous ethnic groups that constituted the majority of the population. This situation finally precipitated a military revolt in 1980 led by a native of non-American descent to overthrow the system that had held sway over Liberia since 1847, and consequently ending the first republic and the political dominance of Americo-Liberians. The new order ushered in by the military revolt did not last long as it paved the way for one of the ghastliest civil wars in Africa, unleashing all the repressed anger and confusion that the people had endured for so long, leading to the total destruction of Liberia. The tragic irony is that Liberia (like Ethiopia, the two oldest independent sates in Africa) eventually imploded in an indescribably painful civil war from which full recovery is yet to come. Let us now turn to G

Ghana

The political independence of Ghana in 1957 is significant in terms of its impact on the rest of the

African continent. Although it was not the first African state to gain independence from colonial domination, it played a very significant role in speeding up independence for other African states from the beginning of the 1960's. At the dawn of Ghana's independence its founder Kwame Nkrumah proclaimed a Pan-African position, linking Ghana's independence to the total liberation and unity of Africa. This position marked the critical difference between Ghana and the earlier independent nations in Africa and as such propelled Ghana into the leadership role championing the demand for African continental unity. Ghana became the haven for African freedom fighters and the unfolding of the practical manifestation of continental African unity, which was expressed in the short-lived union of Ghana, Guinea and Mali.

However, by the end of the first decade of independence the government of Nkrumah and the ideals of a united Africa were largely neutralised by the overthrow of his government in a military coup in 1966. According to the coup leaders the action to overthrow Nkrumah was conducted to rescue Ghanaians from the brutalities of the regime. Much was said and done by the military junta to bolster their justifications for the coup and these included the immediate arrest of members of the ruling political party and non-politicians associated with the government. Furthermore, important publications including books written by Nkrumah were confiscated and burnt, the numerous development projects across the country were closed down and some of the development partners associated with these projects, particularly the Russians and Chinese, were deported from Ghana. In short all the major development plans to industrialise Ghana were immediately terminated.

Writing from Guinea Conakry where he eventually settled after the overthrow of his government, Nkrumah's book *Dark days in Ghana* first published in 1968 exposed the true nature of the military and police dictatorship that seized power, setting the event in the wider continental and world situation. The book is packed with detailed information on the state of Ghana's development and plans for industrialisation before his overthrow. Nkrumah thoroughly demolishes what he called the "big lie" that Ghana had needed to be rescued from "economic chaos". He highlights the systematic sell-off of Ghana's assets to neo-colonialist interest by the junta, and the subsequent reduction of Ghana from a self-respecting sovereign state to the demeaning position of a neo-colony.

Before his eventual overthrow, Nkrumah's political opponents had made numerous attempts on his life, and the cardinal reason for seeking his killing can be explained in terms of his fight for the oppressed Africans to gain their absolute freedom from colonial rule in the shortest possible time. For instance, in an attempt to challenge the legacy of Nkrumah a study (Omari, 1970) portrayed him as an African dictator, describing his rise and desire to transform Africa as an ill-starred crash programme of economic development driven by harsh measures to impose his will on the country. This perspective was popular among the critics of Nkrumah before and after his overthrow. It is important to note that so far Nkrumah is the only Ghanaian head of state to have endured numerous assassination attempts during his tenure.

In spite of the criticisms of his detractors the development projects initiated by Nkrumah's government continue to play a critical role in the daily existence of Ghanaians. For example, the mighty Volta dam continues to supply electricity, and the recent construction of the Bui dam was part of Nkrumah's development plan. Ghana has had several military and civilian regimes but arguably none has been able to succeed in elevating Ghana past the position it occupied in Africa and the world during Nkrumah's rule. After more than half a century since the overthrow of Nkrumah's government, it is now possible to make a comprehensive assessment of the actual development achievement of Ghana beyond the contribution of Nkrumah's government. Such a report will help to shed light on the state of Ghana's progress.

Nigeria

With the largest population in Africa and growing, Nigeria[2] is the most populous state in Africa with well over six times the population of Ghana. Considering its huge population and natural resources, Nigeria can reasonably be described as the powerhouse of Africa and as such, ought to provide the leadership needed in Africa.

Nigeria gained independence from Britain in 1960 and declared itself a Federal Republic in 1963. The hopes of independence and peaceful nation building were soon suspended by a military coup and counter coup in 1966. These coups led to a brutal civil war that erupted in 1967. Popularly known as the Biafra War and commanded by the Igbos in a secessionist attempt along the existing insidious tribal cleavages to break up the fragile federation on which the newly independent nation of Nigeria stood. The war ended in 1970 with

---

[2] See World Bank 2012 at http://www.worldbank.org/en/country/nigeria

close to a million lives lost, a shattered reputation and a nation burdened by deep social and psychological wounds.

For two decades or so after the civil war military coups came to dominate the political landscape of Nigeria and such conditions meant that vital institutions for development and progress had difficulties in taking root. Legendary stories of corruption in Nigeria abound, accentuating the difficulties in nation building. The celebrated Nigerian writer Chinua Achebe (1983), was very clear as to where the problem in Nigeria emanates:

> The trouble with Nigeria is simply and squarely a failure of leadership. There is nothing basically wrong with the Nigerian character. There is nothing wrong with the Nigerian land or climate or water or air or anything else. The Nigerian problem is the unwillingness or inability of its leaders to rise to the responsibility, to the challenge of personal example, which are the hallmarks of true leadership (p1).

Achebe's frustration with the Nigerian leadership is based on his belief that "Nigeria is a nation favoured by Providence" to play a leading role in the world considering its vast material resources and as such sees corrupt leaders and government officials as betraying Nigeria's high destiny.

Corruption continues to persist and according to the United Nations Human Development Report[3] despite its resources, Nigeria is ranked among the counties with the lowest Human Development Index. The poverty in the North of Nigeria is in stark contrast to the more

---

[3] The current estimate of the Nigerian population is about 168,833,776 million. See information on the Nigerian population at: http://hdr.undp.org/en/statistics/

developed southern states. While in the oil-rich southeast, the inhabitants of Delta and Akwa Ibom complain that all the wealth generated in their community flows to Lagos and Abuja. As summed up by Achebe, Nigeria is not beyond change, but can change if leaders who have the will, the ability and the vision emerge. Herein lies the monumental challenge.

Congo

The Democratic Republic of Congo shares some similarities with Nigeria particularly in terms of the abundance of natural resources, however Congo is much larger. Situated almost at the centre of the African continent, the state of Congo epitomises the tragic story of Africans in their struggle to survive the brutal history of the colonial experiences. Crisis followed immediately after political independence came to Congo in June 1960 and by December of the same year the Prime Minister, Patrice Lumumba was arrested and murdered within two months of his arrest. Thus began a new phase in the painful realities of needless death and destruction long before independence to the present time for an African nation that is otherwise endowed with great natural resources to create much prosperity and wellbeing for its people. In other words, Congo has known very little peace from the onset of its birth as a self-governing community under indigenous rule and the future prospects look equally frightful as signs of further violent power struggle between warlords persist.

Today, Congo can be described as a failed state in spite of its potential wealth. The vision of an independent Congo as expressed by Patrice Lumumba in his unscheduled speech[4] as the first democratically elected Prime Minister was full of hope, although this was reported[5] as an offensive speech in the presence of the King of Belgium. The importance of the speech justifies its entire reproduction:

> Men and women of the Congo,
>
> Victorious fighters for independence, today victorious, I greet you in the name of the Congolese Government. All of you, my friends, who have fought tirelessly at our sides, I ask you to make this June 30, 1960, an illustrious date that you will keep indelibly engraved in your hearts, a date of significance of which you will teach to your children, so that they will make known to their sons and to their grandchildren the glorious history of our fight for liberty.
>
> For this independence of the Congo, even as it is celebrated today with Belgium, a friendly country with whom we deal as equal to equal, no Congolese worthy of the name will ever be able to forget that is was by fighting that it has been won, a day-to-day fight, an ardent and idealistic fight, a fight in which we were spared neither privation nor suffering, and for which we gave our strength and our blood.
>
> We are proud of this struggle, of tears, of fire, and of blood, to the depths of our being, for it was a noble and just struggle, and indispensable to put an end to the humiliating slavery which was imposed upon us by force.
>
> This was our fate for eighty years of a colonial regime;

---

[4] The speech was given on Independence Day June 30, 1960. The Belgian king, Boudewijn, opened proceedings by praising the murderous regime of his great-great uncle, Leopold II (millions of Congolese died during his reign from 1885 to 1908), as benevolent, highlighted the supposed benefits of colonialism, and warned the Congolese not to compromise the future with hasty reforms. Lumumba then spontaneously took the podium to deliver his speech, which has become one of the most recognizable statements of anticolonial boldness.

[5] The Guardian newspaper 1st July 1960

our wounds are too fresh and too painful still for us to drive them from our memory. We have known harassing work, exacted in exchange for salaries which did not permit us to eat enough to drive away hunger, or to clothe ourselves, or to house ourselves decently, or to raise our children as creatures dear to us.

We have known ironies, insults, blows that we endured morning, noon, and evening, because we are Negroes. Who will forget that to a black one said "tu", certainly not as to a friend, but because the more honorable "vous" was reserved for whites alone?

We have seen our lands seized in the name of allegedly legal laws which in fact recognized only that might is right.

We have seen that the law was not the same for a white and for a black, accommodating for the first, cruel and inhuman for the other.

We have witnessed atrocious sufferings of those condemned for their political opinions or religious beliefs; exiled in their own country, their fate truly worse than death itself.

We have seen that in the towns there were magnificent houses for the whites and crumbling shanties for the blacks, that a black was not admitted in the motion-picture houses, in the restaurants, in the stores of the Europeans; that a black traveled in the holds, at the feet of the whites in their luxury cabins.

Who will ever forget the massacres where so many of our brothers perished, the cells into which those who refused to submit to a regime of oppression and exploitation were thrown?

All that, my brothers, we have endured.

But we, whom the vote of your elected representatives have given the right to direct our dear country, we who have suffered in our body and in our heart from colonial oppression, we tell you very loud, all that is henceforth ended.

The Republic of the Congo has been proclaimed, and our country is now in the hands of its own children.

Together, my brothers, my sisters, we are going to begin a new struggle, a sublime struggle, which will lead our country to peace, prosperity, and greatness.

Together, we are going to establish social justice and make sure everyone has just remuneration for his labor.

We are going to show the world what the black man can do when he works in freedom, and we are going to make of the Congo the centre of the sun's radiance for all of Africa.

We are going to keep watch over the lands of our country so that they truly profit her children. We are going to restore ancient laws and make new ones which will be just and noble.

We are going to put an end to suppression of free thought and see to it that all our citizens enjoy to the full the fundamental liberties foreseen in the Declaration of the Rights of Man.

We are going to do away with all discrimination of every variety and assure for each and all the position to which human dignity, work, and dedication entitles him.

We are going to rule not by the peace of guns and bayonets but by a peace of the heart and the will.

And for all that, dear fellow countrymen, be sure that we will count not only on our enormous strength and immense riches but on the assistance of numerous foreign countries whose collaboration we will accept if it is offered freely and with no attempt to impose on us an alien culture of no matter what nature.

In this domain, Belgium, at last accepting the flow of history has not tried to oppose our independence and is ready to give us their aid and their friendship, and a treaty has just been signed between our two countries, equal and independent. On our side, while we stay vigilant, we shall respect our obligations, given freely.

Thus, in the interior and the exterior, the new Congo, our dear Republic that my government will create, will be a rich, free, and prosperous country. But so that we will reach this aim without delay, I ask all of you, legislators and citizens, to help me with all your strength.

I ask all of you to forget your tribal quarrels. They exhaust us. They risk making us despised abroad.

I ask the parliamentary minority to help my Government through a constructive opposition and to limit themselves strictly to legal and democratic channels.

I ask all of you not to shrink before any sacrifice in order to achieve the success of our huge undertaking.

In conclusion, I ask you unconditionally to respect the life and the property of your fellow citizens and of foreigners living in our country. If the conduct of these foreigners leaves something to be desired, our justice will be prompt in expelling them from the territory of the Republic; if, on the contrary, their conduct is good, they must be left in peace, for they also are working for our country's prosperity.

The Congo's independence marks a decisive step towards the liberation of the entire African continent.

Sire, Excellences, [Ladies and Gentlemen], my dear fellow countrymen, my brothers of race, my brothers of struggle-- this is what I wanted to tell you in the name of the Government on this magnificent day of our complete independence.

Our government, strong, national, popular, will be the health of our country.

I call on all Congolese citizens, men, women and children, to set themselves resolutely to the task of creating a prosperous national economy which will assure our economic independence.

Glory to the fighters for national liberation!

Long live independence and African unity!

Long live the independent and sovereign Congo![6]

Whatever ones view of the speech, Lumumba's desire to recall the painful experiences of his people with a plea to restore their dignity may be glimpsed in Hochschild's (2006) vivid account of the cruel exploitation of the Congo in his book *King Leopold's Ghost*. Sadly, this speech may have contributed to the strengthening of the forces that eventually destroyed Lumumba and consequently plunged the newly independent Congo into total chaos, which after more than five decades later can only be described as a tragic case. In his insightful book *Challenge of the Congo*, Nkrumah (2002) provided a case study of how foreign exploitation contributed to the destruction of Congo.

South Africa

The history of South Africa has been in large part one of deeply damaging racial divisiveness fuelled in ways similar to the exploitative forces that operated in Congo. However, today South Africa can also be seen as journeying through massive obstacles in its transformational dreams toward a single united state with a common purpose.

Since 1994 South Africa transitioned from the system of apartheid to one of democratic majority rule providing

---

[6] View info at http://www.friendsofthecongo.org/speeches.html

the opportunity for the majority to form a government of national unity under the presidency of Nelson Mandela. In spite of the political changes, the post-apartheid struggle for equality still has far to go in terms of wealth redistribution and human development.

In addition to the social and economic challenges facing South Africa, the destructive nature of the sexually transmitted disease known as the Human immunodeficiency virus / acquired immunodeficiency syndrome (HIV/AIDS) is yet to be fully tackled. It is well known that HIV/AIDS causes illness and death among mature adults who are ironically, the most productive group in any society and in doing so families are destroyed, children for example are often orphaned and their future livelihoods face potential disarray.

The disease has indeed hit Africa the hardest (Barnett and Whiteside, 2006). In the recent UN AIDS report (2012) South Africa still has the highest number of people in the world living with HIV, approximately 5.6 million, or more than 10% of the entire population. Analysis of the impact of AIDS on orphanhood in South Africa estimated that there could be as many as 5.7 million children who will have lost at least one parent by 2015 (Johnson and Dorrington, 2001); and this corresponds to about one third of all the children in the country. Although much work is now being done to fight the disease the future effects of this catastrophic condition are yet to be fully felt.

Egypt

Egypt and South Africa share the distinguishing feature of occupying the northern and southern tips of the

African continent, but differ considerably in their political experiences. Egyptian nationalism gained much momentum after the revolution in 1952 that brought Gamal Abdel Nasser to power. Under Nasser, Egypt become the leader of the Arab world and assumed the role of promoting Pan Arab unity. Nasser not only played a pivotal role in Arab politics but also equally contributed to African solidarity by acknowledging Egypt's African heritage.

The government of Nasser was secular in nature, which generated much resentment particularly from the religious political group, the Moslem Brotherhood, which is a movement with the sole aim of establishing an Islamic state in Egypt. An assassination attempt on the life of Nasser by the Brotherhood resulted in the immediate outlawing of the group and the beginning of a long and complex struggle between Nasser and the Brotherhood. Meanwhile, during this period the standard of living for the common people improved under Nasser's socialistic government until his death from natural causes in 1970.

Anwar Sadat succeeded Nasser as the new ruler of Egypt. Sadat reinstated the Moslem Brotherhood as a tolerated organisation and welcomed them back into Egypt. Ironically, an offshoot Islamic group of the Muslim Brotherhood assassinated Sadat in 1981 as a result of his accommodation of Israel. Hosni Mubarak replaced Sadat and throughout his presidency, the Brotherhood remained essentially illegal until his removal in 2011.

The beginning of 2011 saw the eruption of protests throughout Egypt targeting the downfall of the administration of President Hosni Mubarak and within weeks Mubarak's resignation was announced followed immediately by nationwide celebrations. Thus began a new page in Egypt's long history, one that the tens of thousands who participated in the protests looked forward to a better life. But two years after the downfall of Mubarak, protests continue against the newly elected government for pursuing Islamic fundamentalist ideals under the heavy influence of the Muslim Brotherhood that for decades had been kept out of political participation in Egypt. In 2013 amid the growing political violence in Egypt the Moslem Brotherhood as a consequence has once again been driven into concealment.

The future of Egypt and what the protests mean for those seeking a new democratic beginning is now very difficult to ascertain as this notion has come to mean different things for different groups with particular regard for those seeking an Islamic State and those in favour of a secular State. The situation however provides a unique opportunity for the re-examination and appreciation of the connections of the present Egyptian world to its ancient African roots.

Diaspora Africa

Beyond Egypt and the rest of the physical frontiers of Africa we find the dispersed people of African descent. Diaspora Africa can be described as a nation consisting of the descendants of Africans recently dispersed[7] throughout the world as a result of slavery or forced

---

[7] It is useful to note that as evidence grows regarding Africa being the ancestral home of modern humans over millions of years ago as indicated by Wells (2003), the reference to people (or person) of African descent in our discussions is in relation to movements in recent (thousands of years) history.

removal from their homelands in Africa. While this description of Diaspora Africa may be understood as an abstract idea, its acknowledgement is important in any comprehensive and meaningful discussion of continental Africa.

However, there have been instances in history where the revolutionary zeal and desire to be free from slavery have led enslaved Africans to proclaim and defend their freedom. The first group of people of African descent in the Western hemisphere that succeeded in defeating their masters and the major European powers including the great Napoleon Bonaparte's French army christened their territory Haiti in 1804.

Furthermore, it must be noted that numerous slave revolts erupted throughout the history of the African slave trade in both the Eastern and Western hemispheres, and while most of these revolts were crushed some survived and developed into small self-sustaining communities such as the settlement known today as Yanga in Mexico, which was founded by the African slave revolt leader Gasper Yanga in 1630.

Nevertheless, the importance of Haiti in Pan African history rests on the fact that it was the first republic in the world to be led by people of African descent in gaining such status by revolutionary means. However, since its proclamation of independence Haiti has been ravaged by political violence throughout its centuries old history. Today, it is ranked among the poorest countries in the world. Significant questions remain to be answered concerning the kinds of lessons that can be drawn from the Haitian revolution to inform the African future.

Politics of Betrayal

As already established, the African world can be understood as consisting of Africans on the continent and those of African descent in the Diaspora. Consequently, the various politically independent states discussed above belong to the African world and furthermore, they all demonstrate to lesser or greater degree issues concerning institutional structures that call for major improvements for the effective management of such chronic problems as abject poverty, challenges of human and material sustainable development and above all corruption. There are those who take serious offence when corruption, for example, is highlighted as a grave and debilitating issue across the Africa world by responding to the charge that corruption is not the sole preserve of Africans. Yes, this observation is granted, but does it justify the severely persistent lack of accountability that surrounds the practice in the Africa world? How will Africans find the essential stability to aid the much-needed reconstruction without the effective handling of corruption? Who will lead Africans to secure their redemption? When must this situation be directly confronted?

In tackling the subject of corruption in Africa and its impact on the lives of ordinary Africans, it is important that we scrutinise how foreign loans and capital flight[8] have helped to drain Africa (Nkidumana and Boyce, 2011). For decades diverse methods have been used to channel funds from foreign loans to African governments into private pockets and it is estimated that by 2008 the cumulative wealth of some individual

---

[8] Capital flight may refer to the rapid flow of money or assets out of a country. In the African context this also involves the diversion of government loans into private pockets or bank accounts.

Africans in foreign banks reached the staggering amount of $944 billion. The possible linkages between capital flights and the exploitation of natural resources in some of the oil rich African states is at the heart of the investigations by some writers on oil production and corruption in Africa.

Shaxson (2008) draws our attention to oil production in Africa and the paradoxical nature of the chronic poverty in some of the wealthiest oil producing states such as Nigeria, Equatorial Guinea, Gabon and Angola.   These awful living conditions are generated and fuelled by the rampant corruption endemic in the oil trade when earnings that could be used to lift the poor from deprivation due to the effects of colonialism and exploitation are diverted into private accounts by the ruling elites and furthermore, some of the loot sadly provides the resource for purchasing weapons to supress any discontentment of the people. Feinstein 's (2011) investigations outlined a devastating account of the rampant greed and unbridled corruption pervading the global arms trade and its impact on Africa:

> Unsurprisingly, Africa has been among the shadow world's most fertile ground. The continent's colonial history, independence struggles, Cold War battles, weak state formations and 'big men' rulers willing to plunder their nations to retain power and enrich themselves have ensured continuous conflict, violence and poverty (p435).

Thus, this is how far Africa has come following the winds of political change that swept through the continent over half a century ago. How would some of the key leaders of the movements that brought about political independence make of the current conditions in the African world? What would be the views of Toussaint L'Ouverture or of Kwame Nkrumah? What about Patrice

Lumumba's opinions? And how would Amilcar Cabral explain the situation?

While all the leaders mentioned above were by various means prematurely neutralised by forces opposed to their objectives, Nkrumah's writings remain exceptionally significant if we are to seriously consider the relevance of his views to the unfolding situations throughout the African world. Sensing the dangers facing the newly formed independent African states, Nkrumah consistently advocated a united Africa from the onset of Ghana's independence and he immediately set to work on the project. At the 1963 African Union meeting of heads of states Nkrumah poured out his soul in the following speech:

> It is said, of course, that we have no capital, no industrial skill, no communications and no internal markets, and that we cannot even agree among ourselves how best to utilise our resources.

> Yet all the stock exchanges in the world are preoccupied with Africa's gold, diamonds, uranium, platinum, copper and iron ores. Our capital flows out in streams to irrigate the whole system of Western economy. Fifty-two per cent of the gold in Fort Knox at this moment, where the U. S. A. stores its bullion, is believed to have originated from our shores. Africa provides more than 60 per cent of the world's gold. A great deal of the uranium for nuclear power, of copper for electronics, of titanium for supersonic projectiles, of iron and steel for heavy industries, of other minerals and raw materials for lighter industries - the basic economic might of the foreign Powers - come from our continent.

> Experts have estimated that the Congo basin alone can produce enough food crops to satisfy the requirements of nearly half the population of the whole world.

For centuries Africa has been the milk cow of the Western world. It was our continent that helped the Western world to build up its accumulated wealth.

It is true that we are now throwing off the yoke of colonialism as fast as we can, but our success in this direction is equally matched by an intense effort on the part of imperialism to continue the exploitation of our resources by creating divisions among us.

When the colonies of the American Continent sought to free themselves from imperialism in the 18th century there was no threat of neo-colonialism in the sense in which we know it today. The American States were therefore free to form and fashion the unity which was best suited to their needs and to frame a constitution to hold their unity together without any form of interference from external sources. We, however, are having to grapple with outside interventions. How much more, then do we need to come together in the African unity that alone can save us from the clutches of neo-colonialism.

He went on to say:

If we do not approach the problems in Africa with a common front and a common purpose, we shall be haggling and wrangling among ourselves until we are colonized again and become the tools of a far greater colonialism than we suffered hitherto.

Unite we must. Without necessarily sacrificing our sovereignties, big or small, we can, here and now, forge a political union based on Defence, Foreign Affairs and Diplomacy, and a common Citizenship, an African currency, an African Monetary Zone and an African Central Bank. We must unite in order to achieve the full liberation of our continent. We need a common Defence system with an African High Command to ensure the stability and security of Africa.

We have been charged with this sacred task by our own people, and we cannot betray their trust by failing them. We will be mocking the hopes of our people if we show the slightest hesitation or delay by tackling realistically this question of African Unity[9].

Decades after Nkrumah's speech, the founder of Tanzania Julius Nyrere was humble enough to make a confession:

> The confession is that we of the first generation leaders of independent Africa have not pursued the objective of African unity with the vigour, commitment and sincerity that it deserved[10].

The simple truth that cannot now be easily refuted is that African leaders have deeply disappointed their people. This tragic disappointment is borne in the virulent politics of betrayal deep in the soul of the African body politic.

Nkrumah's pleas for unity and warnings about its absence are turning into bitter realities today. The continuing lack of commitment to a strong continental unity on the one hand has resulted in the collective weakness of Africa on the international stage, and on the other hand, the inability to provide durable solutions to the grinding poverty, senseless violence and the harrowing conflicts that afflict the millions of poor Africans trying to eke out a living in various states of hopelessness. The stampede for independence that began in the middle of the twentieth century now appears to have lost its purpose in delivering a better life for all Africans. Consequently, the African people can expect to face a harsher reality in time to come with leaders who are not absolutely committed to positively supporting the realisation of their full potentialities by seeking ways to create an alternative existence to

---

[9] View info at http://summits.au.int/en/21stsummit/speeches/1963
[10] New African, 26 July 2012

balance the continuing foreign domination of the African World.

CHAPTER TWO

THE OCCIDENTAL EMBRACE

The power of the Western universe over Africa has proved to be an enduring one as Africa continues to exist within the European worldview. After the rapid gaining of freedom across the African continent and the promise of new beginnings, not a single independent African state has been able to develop a productive perspective on African development.

Uneasy Consent

Let us take Ghana as an example. The struggle for Ghana's independence is well known. However, even before Ghana's independence there were those who opposed the granting of such independence as (Ghana was by this time a colony known as the Gold Coast) proposed by the Convention People's Party, which was administering the colony. To highlight their objection, and sensing their impending failure, the Opposition group spearheaded by the National Liberation Movement travelled to Britain to ask the British Secretary of State for the Colonies, Lennox-Boyd, to use whatever influence he had left to secure alterations in the Gold Coast constitution to bring it in line with their designs. Their leader, Dr K.A. Busia at his press conference in London went even further to suggest the setting up of a Royal Commission to investigate the matter[11].   As narrated by Nkrumah (1957), the Gold Coast for Busia was not yet ready for parliamentary democracy and he pleaded with the British:

> We still need you in the Gold Coast...
> Your experiment there is not complete. Sometimes I wonder why you seem in a hurry to wash your hands off us (p279).

Busia's efforts to thwart Ghana's historic stride to independence planned for 6th March 1957 failed. His expression epitomised the power of the European colonial experience at the threshold of the colony's assumption of full responsibility for its own affairs[12].

The support given by external forces for the destruction of Nkrumah's government in Ghana was a widespread pattern across Africa, which, as a consequence, deprived the continent of some of its most competent leaders[13].
The link between the Colonial powers and their colonies in Africa was particularly expressed in the level of commerce that was maintained.   The protracted and complex trade in African resources constituted a major

---

[11] West Africa Magazine, September 15, 1956

[12] Though much as the Colonial administration in the Gold Coast was eager to hand over power to a more conservative indigenous government as represented by Busia's group, their repeated rejection at the polls by the electorate forced the granting of Ghana's independence and the transfer of power to Nkrumah's government. However, the overthrow of Nkrumah by dissident army and police personnel, which was promptly hailed by Western governments, resulted in Busia's eventual rise to power in 1969.

[13] Significant leaders such as Patrice Lumumba, Amilcar Cabral, Mehdi Ben Barka and Felix Moumié became casualties of such support. Soon after the wave of independence across Africa, coup d'états became very fashionable and numerous democratically elected governments were overthrown thus impeding the development of these young democratic states. The impact of the period of deformation that ensued still remains to be fully remedied.

element in the direction and growth in the commerce between the coloniser and the colonised. The exploitation of African labour and resources by colonial companies led to an imbalance that fed into the uneasy consent for the subsequent freedom demanded by the Africans. A notable example is Union Minière, which operated in Congo.

Union Minière[14]

During the numerous decades of its operations, Union Minière du Haut Katanga (UMHK) generated colossal wealth for its shareholders in Belgium and Britain while it harshly exploited the human and natural resources of the Congo. Cheap labour for the mines was assured but challenging to meet the demand as it often exceeded the supply that the sparsely populated mining region could offer. Recruitment of workers from outside the Congo was inevitable and the situation was severe enough for the consideration of indentured labourers from as far as China. However, issues such as the serious gambling

---

[14] Union Minière du Haut Katanga (UMHK) was a mining company formed in 1906 to exploit the mineral wealth of Congo. It came into being as a result of the merger of the Comité Spécial du Katanga (CSK) the Belgian organisation that directed the exploitation of the Congolese lands and a British mining company called Tangayika Concessions Ltd. UMHK became one of the largest capitalist mining conglomerates to emerge from the European colonisation of Africa. It also became one of the world's leading producer of copper, and not only was it the world's most important producer of germanium (used as a semi-conductor in transistors and various electronic devices), it was also the largest producer of cobalt and radium. Furthermore, the mineral deposits of tin, uranium and zinc were among the richest in the world. The mineral resources that came out of the mines significantly contributed to fuelling the industrial might of the Western powers. They played a role in the two great wars the world has experienced. During the First World War, copper from the mines went into the production of bullets and other explosives that assisted the allied forces to win. They also provided the world's best high-grade uranium that went into the making of the atomic bombs that ended the Second World War.

tendencies and prevalence of sodomy among the Chinese brought pressure to end the experiment (Katzenellenbogen, 1975). The labour problem became so acute that a new approach involving a shift from the general policy of using Africans on short-term basis to one of stabilising the workforce was instituted, and from about the mid 1920s onwards, migrant workers were encouraged to settle with their families in the mining camps. The company's labour policy even went as far as to organise marriages between women in the villages and unmarried employees in the mining camps. The intention however, was far from benevolent as managers wanted to breed the company's own supply of labour (Fetter, 1983).

The exploitation of the Africans and their lands continued ferociously in spite of their occasional revolts driven by their wretched living and working conditions. The eagerness to safeguard its operations and source of revenue resulted in UMHK's support for the secessionist Katanga government of Moise Tshombe when the Congo was rashly decolonised in 1960. UMHK continued its mining operations throughout the ensuing disintegration of the country as a result of repeated armed conflicts that plagued the country after independence. After its nationalisation by the Mobutu government in 1966, remnants of UMHK survived to form part of the company now called Umicore. The tenacity of Union Miniere to ruthlessly exploit both the human and natural resources of Africa was typical of the colonial companies that emerged on the continent.

Business Models

The rise of European colonialism in Africa is a thoroughly scrutinised experience that needs no further introduction and therefore, the briefest outline will suffice for our discussion. While Europeans have had a very long association with Africans the occupation, control and imposition of formal rule of European laws over Africa gained prominence from the late nineteenth century onwards as a result of the intense competition among European nations (popularly known as the Scramble for Africa between 1884 and 1910) to expand their national sphere of power and wealth. Feelings and ideologies of civilisation and racial superiority vividly captured in Kipling's poem, *The White Man's Burden*, fired the justifications for the colonial pursuit. Once claims to territories were made and boundaries arbitrarily confirmed, four broad methods of governing these newly acquired territories emerged.

1) Private Companies
The European nations allowed the formation of private companies that were granted large territories to administer in Africa. Entrepreneurs who were interested in exploiting the natural resources of the territories were allowed to govern through their companies. In order to do so successfully, they were allowed to establish their own system of taxation and labour recruitment. For example, the British South Africa Company was formed in 1887 under the control of Cecil Rhodes. Using force and coercion the company colonized three territories in south-central Africa namely, Nyasaland (Malawi), Northern Rhodesia (Zambia), and Southern Rhodesia (Zimbabwe). The Company governed these colonies until 1923. Similarly,

the British East Africa Company was established in 1888 and only lasted until 1893.

2) Direct Rule

Under this system of governance, the Europeans did not try to negotiate with the indigenous African rulers and governments as their authorities were given a subordinate role in these administrations. The abiding principle was that of assimilating the African into the European culture by implementing policies that weakened indigenous power networks and institutions. This model was the preferred choice of the French, Germans, Portuguese and Belgians.

3) Indirect Rule

This system of governance favoured by the British used indigenous African rulers within the colonial administration albeit in an inferior role. Generally, it was a more cooperative but no better model than direct rule as it increased divisions between indigenous communities.

4) Settler Rule

By this model European settlers made the colonies their permanent home and imposed direct rule on them. In order to thrive in these colonies, settlers demanded special political and economic rights and privileges. The settler rule was characterized by its severe policies toward the indigenous Africans as the prosperity of the settlers depended on economic exploitation and political oppression of the African population that vastly outnumbered them.

The profitability of doing business in Africa particularly in the mining and agricultural sectors provided the key motivational factor for the yearning and persistence of

Colonial powers to continue to maintain their influence even after the giddy period of struggle for independence by Africans. Nevertheless, in some parts of the continent such as in the former Portuguese colonies, it took an all-out war of liberation for the achievement of their independence. And in parts of Southern Africa the European settlers declared their independence in the hope that they can prevent the rule of the African majority.

Changes have come to pass and the European colonies and settler communities have given way to the rule by Africans. However, the legacy of the European colonial domination has left an indelible mark on the African psyche that continues to impact on the development of the continent.

Meaningful Relationship

The timeless, intimate but uneasy relationship between Europe and Africa is in many ways defined by the shared experiences. While the point about the abuse that Africans have suffered after centuries of subjugation has been extensively examined, it is useful to restate how it deeply characterises the European–African relationship.

Nature of the Relationship

Franz Fanon (1993) made a significant contribution to our understanding of the nature of the relationship between the African and the European as a consequence of colonisation. Fanon offered some insights into the general effects of the psychology of racism and the dehumanisation central to colonial domination. His ideas will be given further attention later but for now let us use draw on him as an inspiration to enquire about the coloniser. What are the effects of the colonisation of Africa on the European? To what extent do these factors continue to impact on the European relations with the African?

The dehumanising and destructive effects of colonialism are not only experienced by the colonised as noted by Aimé Césaire (2000):

> First we must study how colonization works to *decivilize* the colonizer, to *brutalize* him in the true sense of the word, to degrade him, to awaken him to buried instincts, to covetousness, violence, race hatred, and moral relativism; and we must show that . . . each time a little girl is raped and in France they accept the fact, each time a Madagascan is tortured and in France they accept the fact, civilization acquires another dead weight, a universal regression takes place, a gangrene sets in, a centre of infection begins to spread; and that at the end of all these treaties that have been violated, all these lies that have been propagated, all these punitive expeditions that have been tolerated, all these prisoners who have been tied up and "interrogated," all these patriots who have been tortured, at the end of all the racial pride that has been encouraged, all the boastfulness that has been displayed, a poison has been distilled into the veins of Europe and, slowly but surely, the continent proceeds toward *savagery* (pp35-36).

This savagery is revealed in the supreme barbarism that underpinned Nazism, and before Europeans became its victims they were its accomplices. In other words, before the brutality of Nazism was inflicted upon Europe it was tolerated and legitimised in its applications to non-European peoples as observed by Césaire:

> Yes, it would be worthwhile to study clinically, in detail, the steps taken by Hitler and Hitlerism and to reveal to the very distinguished, very humanistic, very Christian bourgeois of the twentieth century that without his being aware of it, he has a Hitler inside him, that Hitler *inhabits* him, that Hitler is his *demon*, that if he rails against him, he is being inconsistent and that, at bottom, what he cannot forgive Hitler for is not *the crime* in itself, *the crime against man*, it is not *the humiliation of man as such*, it is the crime against the white man, the humiliation of the white man, and the fact that he applied to Europe colonialist procedures which until then had been reserved exclusively for the Arabs of Algeria, the "coolies" of India and the "niggers" of Africa (ibid, p36)

Césaire's stance is very challenging yet very helpful in allowing us to engage in an honest discussion concerning the shame that the sincere, truth-seeking European must encounter. Similarly, Lindqvist (2002) fearlessly confronts some of these issues highlighted by Césaire from an interesting perspective that is simultaneously a travel guide and a historical examination of European imperialism and racism spanning the last two centuries.

While the official colonial and mainstream European outlook had nothing but contempt for Africans as a consequence of their subjugation, there were some European voices that cried out against the overwhelming cruelty that Africans suffered. One such voice was Joseph Booth, the British missionary whose pronouncements led to his banishment from the colonies. While other missionaries either actively encouraged or passively observed the colonial expansion and brutalities, Booth (1897) spoke out against the mistreatment of Africans:

> During the past three centuries the African's progress has doubtless been greatly retarded by the ungenerous and often criminal treatment he was awarded by his European neighbours. As these latter emerged from barbarism and entered upon a period of commercial and territorial enterprise, discovering and seizing upon new countries, subduing and often destroying their inhabitants, they ruthlessly set to work to people some of these countries with slaves plundered from the coast of Africa, and thus inaugurated one of the most, if not absolutely the most gigantic and long sustained crimes of modern times. To supply this accursed demand for slave labour, the coastal Africans were primed to prey upon the tribes of the interior, and thus the hands of the Africans were kept constantly imbued in each other's blood.

> The British, Portuguese, Dutch and Spanish were the most prominent in this nefarious traffic of human flesh. The proposal of the European was thus to appropriate the person and labour of the African.

> So enormous and long sustained a wrong, though clung to with almost fiendish tenacity by the interested class, was doomed to be abandoned before the growing power of unfettered Christian teaching, and this colossal injustice received its final death blow by means of the great American civil war, which forever burst asunder the fetters of the Negro slave.

> But the unhallowed spirit of European greed for aggrandizement at the African's expense was not, though sorely wounded, to die so speedy a death. The flagrant and revolting nature of the old method must perforce be abandoned: but the resolve to exploit the African in some form yet remained.

> As the wonderful resources of his country became known, and the treasures of precious stones, gold and agriculture products were revealed, the desire to posses the property of the African, rather than his person, became manifest. The European scramble for the African's land then began in

earnest. The purpose of certain European powers to appropriate large sections of African territory, was, however, cleverly glossed over, more or less, with a philanthropic film.

The slave trading, which at one time these same powers had industriously fostered and which the Arab still prosecuted, was now to be extirpated by the wholesale appropriation of territory and the subduing of the inhabitants.

The partition, or plunder of Africa by this concerted agreement, or conspiracy, of certain European powers, was conveniently arranged, and the closing decade of the nineteenth century witnessed the SECOND MANIFICENTLY UNSCRUPOLUS proposal of the European to exploit his African neighbour. The former clumsy proposal to annex and transplant the African's person was costly, cumbersome and infamous; the present proposal to purloin the land under his feet and adroitly to utilize the African as an instrument to disclose, develop and deposit its resources for the European's benefit, is the self-same in spirit, but more ingeniously dressed, further reaching in its effects, and far less likely to be challenged (pp9-10)

He goes on to say

As "righteousness exalteth a nation," so does righteousness exalt the individual in God's sight. If we cannot persuade the rulers of, or the heterogeneous mass of thinkers which composes a nation to act righteously even generously; as individuals we can stand out separately and touch not the unclean thing of national plunder and oppression (p20)

What is abundantly clear is the uncompromising position Booth adopted, driven to this point by the shamefulness he felt for the widespread exploitation of the African, which he could no longer accept regardless of the consequences before him. In view of the wrath facing any dissenting voice, his plea unsurprisingly went unheeded. Memmi (1967) gives us a brilliant analysis and condition of the colonizer who refuses to accept the injustice of colonization.

> If he persists, he will learn that he is launching into an undeclared war with his own people which will always remain alive, unless he returns to the colonialist fold or is defeated. Wonder has been expressed at the vehemence of colonizers against any among them who put colonization in jeopardy. It is clear that such a colonizer is nothing but a traitor. He challenges their very existence and endangers the very homeland which they represent in the colony (p65)

Such must have been the burden on Booth to terminate his resistance to the existing colonial policies and widespread practices of the day. Notwithstanding his own personal tragedies Booth never wavered and continued his campaign until his death in 1932, and exactly one hundred years later some of the ideas he articulated regarding self-government for the African found expression in the independence of Ghana in 1957.

It is important for us to observe that the position Booth adopted was simply but powerfully to confront the inconsistencies inherent in the colonial relationship between the European and the African. The conduct of Booth reasserts the age-old lesson that continues to be relevant for the individual to be prepared to take on the responsibility of combating injustice whenever and wherever it occurs by any productive means.

Building Trust

Much time has passed since the colonial era officially ended in the second half of the last century, and how may we now evaluate the European–African relationship? To what extent has the colonial mind-set changed towards Africa? In what ways do some of the colonial habits continue to shape the European–African relationship? Is it possible for an enduring and meaningful relationship based on trust and respect to flourish?

African nationalism and resistance to colonialism that led to political freedom throughout the continent dealt a blow to colonial rule that ended it. In this regard, the colonial outlook altered to accept the inevitability of independence demanded by the Africans, a position that was clearly articulated in 1960 by the British Prime Minister Harold Macmillan in his declaration that the wind of change blowing through the African continent at the time was a fact for the British colonial power to accept.

However, gaining political freedom did not necessarily result in economic liberation as the means of production remained with the colonial commercial businesses, and their need to control the natural resources and commercial markets in Africa as indicated by Nkrumah (2002, 2004) contributed to the destabilization that ensued among some of the newly independent African states such as Congo. Consequently, instead of being regarded by the African people as supporters of their aspirations to be free and self-sufficient, distrust for the colonial powers grew among sections of the African population. Furthermore, this distrust intensified as the ideological struggle between capitalism and socialism, which gave meaning to the Cold War, manifested some of its bitterest results in Africa with tragic consequences. The devastation of Africa from the post-colonial period and through the Cold War era continued with the neoliberal perspective, which found expression in the structural adjustment programmes that the continent experienced in the latter half of the twentieth century.

Africa entered the twenty-first century so deeply ravaged that the British Prime Minister Tony Blair in 2001 described the state of poverty in Africa as "a scar on the conscience of the world." Blair's gesture to work with Africans to solve their problems, and his plea to the world to support the effort culminated in the forming of the Commission for Africa in 2004. The task of the commission was to define the challenges facing Africa, and to provide clear recommendations on how to support the changes needed to reduce poverty. A report[15] produced by the commission a year later concluded that a comprehensive action to meet the challenges facing Africa could only be done through a new partnership based on key considerations including mutual respect and solidarity. The significance of the report is that it boldly placed responsibility for tackling poverty in Africa in the hands of Africans, but urged the rest of the world, particularly developed economies to follow their lead by providing resources, through aid and debt cancellation, and furthermore, by ending the damage being done to Africa's fortunes as a result of unfair trade rules, ineffective aid, irresponsible business practices, arms trade and corruption. Although the underpinning ideas of the Commission are not new to Africans, nevertheless it is arguable that Blair's effort has contributed in some ways to advancing a more positive rapport between Africa and Europe. To what extent has the work of the Commission been generally successful?

---

[15] See 'Our Common Interest' at http://www.commissionforafrica.info/2005-report

In 2010 the Commission carried out an assessment[16] of the impact of the original report and concluded by presenting the progress made though much remains the same vis-à-vis African problems. For example, it indicated that there has been much positive progress in Africa since 2005 and the continent may now be on the verge of a period of extraordinary growth and opportunity. But at the same time, Africa, south of the Sahara remains the worlds poorest region with a negligible share of world trade, and with many internal and external obstacles to growth and development. It then urges the international community to provide the extra aid without which Africa is unlikely to meet the Millennium Development Goals (MDGs). The report ends by pressing both African states and the international community to do more to support Africa in challenging the lack of development it faces.

Blair's limited commitment to Africa's development led to his military intervention that contributed significantly to bringing about peace in the war ravaged West African state of Serra Leone. Blair was the first European leader to recognize the significance of Africa in affecting world peace if the continent is not supported to develop its potential, and in doing so contributed in some way to fostering good relationship between Europe and Africa.

The relationship between Europe and Africa is revealing in the arena of trade between the two. After a decade of trade negotiations over economic partnership agreements (EPAs) between Africa and Europe no significant progress has yet been made. What could be the underlying reason? Could it be that Europe is too stuck in its colonial perception of Africa to view Africa as a serious business partner on equal terms? On the other

[16] Commission for Africa. Report 2010: 'Still our common interest'

hand, could it be that Africa has not yet confidently demonstrated the capacity to handle its affairs in a manner that will send a clear signal to the world in order to command the respect it deserves? For example, recent events in Africa such as the civil wars in Sierra Leone and Ivory Coast to some extent relied on British and French troops to end the conflict. Similarly, the removal of Gadhafi as the Libyan leader due to the civil unrest that occurred in Libya involved European assistance to achieve that goal. French forces on behalf of Mali engaged Islamist waging brutal arracks on the Malian people and in the Central African Republic, reliance on French presence was crucial for peace to prevail. Consequentially, the inability of Africans to resolve their internal conflicts and their dependence on foreign assistance have deep ramifications in bolstering longstanding perceptions of Africans and distorting the significance of African independence. On the other hand, how can Africans not feel some sense of gratitude especially by those who were saved from destruction and death as a result of the interventions by Europeans? However, further questions remain for answers in the future. For instance, do these interventions in some remote way begin to provide a basis for the benevolent appearance of European control of Africa and its resources? Will they influence some of the issues regarding unfair trading arrangements with Africa?

Within a section of the African public there remains a residual level of distrust for European or Western engagement with Africa as a result of some entrenched attitudes on both sides. The notion that descendants cannot be responsible for the wrongdoings of their ancestors is defensible. Thus descendants of European colonialists or settlers cannot be readily held accountable for the transgressions of their ancestors.

However, if they actively or passively perpetuate the wrongdoings of their ancestors only then can they become accomplices and as such, equally responsible for sustaining the unacceptable behaviours of the past. As indicated earlier, the relationship between the European world and Africa is deeply intertwined, passing through periods of inequality and great pain and yet the twenty-first century offers abundant opportunities for the reestablishment of genuine relationship based on genuine concern and regard for the other. In this case Nelson Mandela has clearly demonstrated the depth of the African generosity in enduring the vilest conduct of the European and still believe in friendship and harmonious coexistence. Consequently, the burden is now on the European world to rise to Mandela's challenge in changing some of the deeply held European attitudes toward Africa and embrace it in a genuine relationship based on the desire for a deeper understanding and care for the other as demonstrated by Booth and many others. This genuine renewal of the European-African relationship could form a fresh alliance in the face of the great global challenges with regard to resources and security that are shaping global politics and economic trends. On the other hand, for the European world to neglect this opportunity would provide the opening for the Oriental world to offer a new and more intimate relationship with Africa and to this discussion we now turn.

CHAPTER THREE

THE ORIENTAL AFFAIR

T he relationship between Africa and the Oriental (or Eastern) world goes far back into antiquity, long before the arrival of the Europeans in Africa. If we consider the oriental world as encompassing all of the Asiatic people then for the African American scholar Chancellor Williams (1987), the initial presence of the Asians in Africa first concentrated around the delta region of the River Nile in present day Egypt from about 4000 BC. The notion of the 'two lands'[17] that frames our view of Egypt in antiquity and generally expressed as Lower and Upper Egypt can be understood as emanating from the perceived differences between the settlement of Asiatic people in Lower Egypt and the Africans occupying the upper regions of Egypt through which the Nile flows from the heart of Africa into the Mediterranean Sea.

Endless Desires

The relentless invasions by the Asians from the delta area for control of the wealth and resources of the

---

[17] Egypt in antiquity was formed through the unification of the delta region where the Nile empties into the Mediterranean Sea and the hinterland forming the upper region through which the Nile flows.

inland region and the counter offensives by the Africans to retain their control continued for thousands of years; a condition that ultimately contributed to the destruction of the greatest African civilization that emerged along the Nile valley. The invasions took many varied forms ranging from seeking resettlement due to natural disasters elsewhere such as famine, integrating with the indigenous African community, trading and finally the outright declarations of wars, destructions and pillaging. Bypassing the distortions and confusions that have resulted from some of the dominant approaches to the history of Africa, the ascendancy of the Hyksos, Assyrians, Persians and others that followed remain undisputed. If one had a series of political maps of this long period of history, we should have ancient Egypt expanding and contracting like an amœba under a microscope, as summed up by Wells (1922):

> ... we should see these various Semitic states of the Babylonians, the Assyrians, the Hittites and the Syrians coming and going, eating each other up and disgorging each other again (p98).

This period of Asiatic supremacy continued with the Persians until the occupation of Egypt by the Greeks who not merely plundered the wealth and resources of the land, but moved their capital city to Egypt. The decline of the Greeks gave way to Roman ascendancy in Egypt until the emergence of the Arabs.

The Arab Experience

Coming from the East as a new military force in the seventh century and with overt fanaticism to spread the word of Islam, the Arabs overran Egypt and changed the political, cultural and religious map of the region from then on to the present time. However, considering the colossal impact of the Arabs on Africa it is unfortunate that a thorough understanding of the enduring ramifications of their conquest continues to elude a large number of Africans. For example, while the embarrassing matter of the centuries old gruesome Arab slave trade and its attendant degradation of Africans in the Arabian worldview continues to the present in very subtle ways that now needs to be fully and vigorously exposed, some Africans today have taken to the indiscriminate murder of other innocent African men, women and children in the name of Arab-Islam. Is this the true legacy of the Arab conquest in Africa? Who really are the Arabs?

The harsh desert environment went into the physical and psychological making of the Arab (Hitti, 2002), and these attributes forming the core of their nomadic beginnings in the Arabian Peninsula provided the substance for their conquests. The Arab nomad represents the best adaptation of human life to desert conditions and the demarcation between the wandering and sedentary elements in their population is not sharply drawn. The interaction between those who adopted sedentary living to form townships and the desert folk was motivated by the urgent dictates of self-interest and self-preservation. Putting it plainly by Hitti (2002):

> The nomad insists on extracting from his more favourably situated neighbour such resources as he himself lacks, and that either by violence – raids – or by peaceful methods – exchange. He is land pirate or broker, or both at once (p23).

The notions of such raids and its associated terminology were carried over by the Arabians into the Islamic conquests.

The basis of the Arabian nomadic society is the clan and the tent, which is their traditional dwelling place, represents a family. Members of an encampment of a group of tents constitute a clan, and a number of related clans grouped together form a tribe. All members of the same clan submit to the authority of one chief who is the senior member of the clan and consequently, unconditional loyalty is expected between clansmen. Blood relations, real or imagined provided the binding element in such tribal arrangements. In the world of the Arab nomad tribal affiliation is considered supreme and to have none is to be beyond the reach of protection and safety in the hostile desert environment. A stranger may seek such protection by adoption into a family, and in the same way a weaker clan may be protected or incorporated into a stronger clan or tribe. Explaining the entrenchment of the notion of 'aṢabīyah, which can be understood as the spirit of the clan and implying absolute loyalty between clansmen as noted by Hitti (2002):

> This ineradicable particularism in the clan, which is the individualism of the member of the clan magnified, assumes that the clan or tribe as the case may be, is a unit by itself, self-sufficient and absolute, and regards every other clan or tribe as its legitimate victim and object of plunder and murder. Islam made full use of the tribal system for its military purposes. It divided the army into units based on tribal lines, settled the colonists in the conquered lands in tribes and treated new converts from among the subjugated peoples as clients. The unsocial features of individualism and 'aṢabīyah were never outgrown by the Arab character as it developed and unfolded itself after the rise of Islam, and were among the determining factors that led to the disintegration and ultimate downfall of the various Islamic states (pp27–28).

The geographical composition of the Arabian Peninsula is such that the hostile desert divides the land into northern and southern segments and thereby contributing to the seeming variation in the characteristics of the inhabitants. The Northern Arabs are mainly nomads living in tents and the mostly sedentary Southern Arabs inhabit the seaside regions of the south. The Southern Arabs came to prominence first due to their proximity and contact with ancient African civilisations before the rise of the Northern Arabs with Islam to overshadowed them.

Arabs have been recorded in Egyptian history long before the advent of Islam in Africa. In a royal tomb of the first Egyptian dynasty dating from around 3100BC at Abydos, the British Egyptologist Petrie, in 1900 found a portrait on a piece of ivory of a typical Semite labelled "Asiatic" with a long pointed beard presumably a south Arabian. An earlier relief belonging to the same dynasty depicts an emaciated Asiatic nomad chief in a loincloth crouching in submission and about to be destroyed by his Egyptian captor with a mace. What does this event from our remotest past exhibiting the subjugation of the Asiatic by the African over 3000 years before the rise of the Arabs with Islam in Africa tell us? What is evident is that the Arabs could not add much to the ancient Egyptian civilization they eventually overran as it had already suffered centuries of plundering by earlier invasions but proceeded to extract from it as much as possible for their own purposes and so the notion that 'the original Arabs had nothing to teach but everything to learn' was an honest observation made by Hitti (2002). Thus the great pyramids at Giza where stripped of their precision fitted casing blocks to build the mosques in what became the city of Cairo.

How may we account for the legacy of the Arab conquests in Africa? Writers such as the Kenyan historian Ali Mazrui (1975), have sought to present a favourable influence of the Arabs on Africans. Mazrui offers the view that the relationship between the two is such that the Arab is usually the giver and the African the receiver by arguing that throughout the history of the involvement of Arabs in Africa, they have been 'both conquerors and liberators, both traders in slaves and purveyors of new ideas.' While acknowledging the fact that Arabs engaged in slavery for a thousand years, if not more, he is swift to attempt to reduce its impact by drawing attention to the transatlantic slave trade. The enormity and enduring bearing of the Arab slave trade and subjugation of Africans from antiquity to our present time is in urgent need of scrutiny. It remains to be swept from under the Arabian rug and into the light of day for full exposure and rigorous examination, as it has been in the case of the transatlantic slave trade.

Modern historical accounts of the Arabs to a large extent have excluded or remained silent on the African contributions to their rise. For example, in the works by both Hitti (2002), and Hourani (2013), the reader is given the impression, that Egypt bears little relationship with the so called Zanj, which in these works refer to Black African slaves. It is interesting to note the persistence of the notion of the 'two lands' from the remotest time in antiquity to the present day as the Arabs have continued the tradition through their views of Africans. In these historical accounts the Zanj are also used as militias or Eunuchs in the various Arab armies. Williams (1987) however, provides a very different and forceful perspective to Mazrui in his examination of the relationship between the Arabs and the Africans:

Modern Africans and students of Africa have tended to emphasize the destructive impact of European imperialism in Africa while ignoring the most damaging developments from the Arab impact *before* the general European takeover in the last quarter of the nineteenth century, relatively recent period. This point is important. For one of the most remarkable chapters in the history of the Blacks is that dealing with those dauntless leaders and people who, having lost one state after another along with three-fourths of their kinsmen, nevertheless overrode all the forces of destruction and death and began to rebuild, always once again, still another state. From the earliest times the elimination of these states as independent African sovereignties had been an Asian objective, stepped up by Muslim onslaughts after the seventh century A.D. So the re-established black states were still being conquered and Islamized when Europeans began to arrive in great numbers to impose their rule over both Asians and Africans. The big thing that happened here, to repeat, is generally glossed over, ignored or forgotten. The last being a pretension, since a historical development of this magnitude could hardly be forgotten by serious writers on Africa. For what happened, very simply, was that European imperialism in Africa checked and replaced Arab imperialism (p47).

He goes on to say:

The Arab screams against Western imperialism are the screams of outrage against Western imperialism for checking and subduing Eastern imperialism in the very midst of the Blacks they had conquered. There are still countless thousands of Blacks who are naïve enough to believe that the Arabs' bitter attack on the Western colonialism show their common cause with Black Africa (p47).

This analysis in some way highlights the difficulties that Franz Fanon experienced as a Black man identifying with and fighting alongside Algerians for their independence who considered themselves solely as Arabs. Memmi (1973) tries to explain Fanon's predicament in terms of the fact that Black Africans were formerly, as much the slaves of the Arabs as of the Europeans and consequently, the differences between the Arabs and Black Africans remain very problematic and far from being settled. This ancient and deeply rooted contempt for Black Africans resulted in the indiscriminate killings of dark-skinned Africans accused of supporting Gaddafi, the Libyan leader during the recent uprising in Libya. Similarly, the Tuareg terror attacks in neighbouring Mali soon after the Libyan uprising was carried out with impunity in the name of Arab-Islam and complete disregard for the local inhabitants. The Islamic outrages that went on in Sudan and surfacing in Nigeria and the Central African Republic must not be viewed in isolation but must be understood as springing from the same historical conditions as a consequence of the Arab invasion of Africa. If racism against Black Africans in the Arab world is alive and strong today after well over one thousand years of Arab-Islam in Africa then how do we account for its benefits to Africans beyond the all too familiar story of exploitation and degradation? This is an assessment that Africans must seriously undertake for a clearer sense of how they plan to tackle their present difficulties for a better future, one that recognises the eternal attraction of Africa to foreign forces for its resources. This point brings us to the present advances being made by China in Africa.

The Chinese Engagement

The current Chinese presence in Africa and the ensuing forceful wooing of Africans brings us to the discussion of what lies ahead in the future for Africa. The issue raises various critical questions that Africans must consider in view of their past experiences and their enduring legacies. What are the real intentions of China in Africa? What questions should the Africans be asking the Chinese and indeed themselves? What sort of relationship will become of this intoxicating courtship?

Let us begin, as it is always customary, by enquiring about the background of China the suitor. Situated on the far eastern edge of Asia with a large sweep of its boundary along the Pacific Ocean, China remains the most populous nation on Earth. China's ancient and illustrious history progressed through centuries of various ruling dynasties until the collapse of the dynastic system brought about the establishment of the Peoples Republic of China under a communist system of government from the mid twentieth century to the present. The drive for remaking the Chinese society by the Communist government through programmes such as the Great Leap Forward and the Cultural Revolution ended in disasters. However, economic reforms and political curtailment from the late 1970's and after the cold war have led to the rapid growth of the Chinese economy and its subsequent newfound status as a world superpower.

So how did they accomplish such staggering progress after the demise of communism? Since ancient times the Chinese have always demonstrated their determination and resourcefulness from the erection of the great wall to preserve their culture and keep intruders out of China through to the hardships of the cultural revolution instigated by Mao Zedong, the founder of the communist regime of the Peoples Republic of China.

While the Chinese may like to consider their thousands of years old culture as the longest continuous civilization in the world, it is however, not the oldest when compared to Ancient Egypt for example. Anyhow, the Chinese mindfulness and appreciation of their long history is arguably a significant factor in their present development. Even through the bloody years of Mao Zedong's reign when one of the key objectives was to root out old ideas, a kind of suppression of historical memory for supposedly progressive ones based on Marxist-Leninist ideology, was ironically in some ways also informed by favoured periods of their history (Keay, 2009). The sense of history coupled with the determination to redress past humiliations drive the pragmatism with which the Chinese have engaged their problems and the world at large. During the early years of the communist regime, China relied on, and received support from the erstwhile USSR, modelling their industrial, banking and commercial nationalizations on that system in setting the scene for an industrial base which, similar to the Soviet model, was deemed essential for a strong and self sufficient socialism. We can observe, as indicated earlier that at this stage of their political experiment the ideology of the Chinese communist regime was based on European thought as propounded in the political ideas of Marx and Lenin. However, after a series of bitter ideological and territorial disputes China and the USSR later severed relations. Incidentally, a number of territorial disputes have occurred between China and a number of neighbouring countries.

Nearly a decade after the communist ascendancy in 1958, China's Great Leap Forward was launched as an economic and social campaign led by Mao to rapidly transform China from an agrarian economy into an industrialised communist society. However, by 1961 the campaign ended in disaster, resulting in the deaths of tens of millions through what has become known as the Great Chinese Famine[18].

Meanwhile, the growing ideological hostility between China and the USSR forced China to turn to other Asian, Latin American and African countries to form newer alliances and further China's economic and ideological redevelopment. It was soon after this period that the Chinese in 1970 undertook the building of the railroad from Tanzania to Zambia after Western governments declined to support the project. By this time, the Cultural Revolution already launched by Mao in 1966 was in full motion to purge the enemies of the state from Chinese society in order to re-establish his dictatorship, and furthermore to prevent the development of what he perceived to be the bureaucratic, capitalist-style communism of the USSR. This self-imposed restriction, which lasted until 1976, the year in which Mao passed away, also resulted in the final severing of political relations with the USSR and the Western world.

Deng Xiaoping was appointed after the passing of Mao, to oversee the transition of China's planned economy to a semi-capitalist mixed economy, which he consolidated with further commercial and diplomatic relations with the West. Ironically, it was this fear of turning what Mao saw as the peasant communist revolution into a capitalist-style takeover that precipitated the Cultural Revolution and as he correctly anticipated this occurred soon after his death when the government of Deng denounced the Cultural Revolution as a failure. China

---

[18] The famine triggered by the Great Leap Forward was unquestionably the worst in the twentieth century. Fenby (2013), argues that although 30 million is generally accepted as the estimated number of deaths, a secret report, produced decades after the tragic disaster reported more that 40 million deaths.

has since then become a significant contributor in the free capitalist world market and in order to meet some of the demands of its newfound capitalist needs is keen to bring Africa strategically into its field of intentions. The worrying question of China's intentions in Africa is heightened by the tension between its present capitalistic drive as against its past apparent ideological drive during the Mao years.

Ecstasy

The deep penetration of China into Africa is no longer a coy affair but an aggressive and obsessive liaison now unfolding for all to observe, and the perception that this is a one-sided exploitative affair has now led to new study opportunities for scholars to explore. Meanwhile, commentators remain keenly observant of the nature of the affair and its future ramifications. Alden (2007) provides timely analysis of the situation to determine whether this affair would be that of a development partner, economic competitor or new hegemon. Energy resources are the most important focus of China's engagement with Africa and consequently form the major bulk of investments in the region. The economic implications of China's rise as the lead buyer of the world's resources in the context of global supply and demand has transformed it to become the most sought after source of capital investment for both rich and poor countries alike (Moyo, 2012).

China's readiness to fund foreign governments and cater to most needs of host governments particularly those from the poorest countries makes it a more attractive alternative financier than the international financial bodies that often attach their loans to stringent policies.

The willingness of China to easily finance projects in countries administered by legitimate or rogue governments is one of the highly attractive factors why African governments are ecstatic over partnering with China and hence the penetration it now enjoys across the continent with particular regard to its exploitation of Africa's natural resources. China and its investments in Africa are viewed more favourably in many African countries such as in Ghana, Nigeria, South Africa, Ethiopia and Kenya.

Today, in a number of African countries including Ghana, Chinese influence continues to grow as its visibility in terms of financial and technical injections into various sectors of host African economies remain extremely exciting. However, lurking in such unbridled enjoyment of the blossoming relationship for Africa and China are real dangers.

Come Morning

From a global perspective China is doing its best in terms of resource acquisition in order to be well prepared for a possible future where the availability of natural resources can no longer meet our insatiable demand. On the other hand, as a host country for foreign businesses, China is cleverly reluctant to open up its mineral resources for exploitation (Moyo, 2012), and where a foreign company is given the authorization for exploration, if rewards begin to accrue after initial successful exploration then the rights of the company to continue further extraction are severely curtailed in favour of a Chinese takeover. Similarly, the racism and ill treatment that Africans who principally work as traders in China endure is worth noting (Alden, 2007) as their requests to establish a kind of Africatown to mitigate their plight are immediately and absolutely rejected by the Chinese authorities. Meanwhile numerous Chinatowns are taking root on the African continent. Furthermore, Chinese firms and individuals have moved into the domestic African markets to openly compete with local firms and business for trade. In addition to involvement in large-scale projects in areas such as construction and telecommunications, the Chinese are also involved in artisanal mining, petty trading, mainly buying and selling of foodstuffs in local market squares, taking up contracts to supply food to hospitals and many other small businesses reserved and protected by laws for local business to perform.

The Chinese approach to Africa is done in three ways (Alden, 2007): the multilateral way whereby Africa is dealt with as a whole as demonstrated for example in the China-African summits where heads of state are summoned to Beijing and the funding of a new African Union building in Addis Abba to cement the relationship; the bilateral way whereby China deals separately with individual African states in various government-to-government agreements and undertakings; the regional way, whereby twinning provinces and free trading zones are created for firms to trade within the local economies. Such inroads into Africa by China raise truly disturbing questions concerning the future and what the outcome will be for Africans. Some commentators such as Chan (2013) argue that there are various common assumptions in the literature on China and Africa that are deceptive, for which an attempt to provide a different perspective is made in outlining the Chinese approach and misconceptions about the Chinese involvement in Africa.

The debate, if any, regarding China's activities in Africa is highly contentious as on the one hand there are those who are reasonably alarmed by the ease with which China is seen to invest in Africa without strict regard for international guidelines and formalities extending from good governance to social and environmental implications for host countries, and on the other hand, those who are positively supportive of such easy access to badly needed finance for host countries. While such debates will go on, what is of great concern is that what China will do or not do in Africa in the future is definitely unknown to anyone including the Chinese as this is predicated on future events. Consequently, arguments and various pronouncements about the future of China-Africa relations are predominantly theoretical and suspect. This situation becomes sharply focused when viewed through the continuing unstable economic and political conditions unfolding under the global free market system where power, exploitation and greed remain supreme. Thus today, it is in the interest of the Chinese and arguably so, to say or do absolutely anything to attempt to secure their future as best as they can. The worrying question regarding Africa is – how prudently are the Africans thinking and preparing as a people for their long-term future?

Mindful Associations

The Oriental (or Eastern) world draws much on the colonial past and continuing dominance of the Western world as a symbolic starting point for closer cooperation and partnership between the Africans and the Orientals. While these symbolic gestures had powerful connotations through the years of struggle for independence and soon after in Africa and Asia, can the same be said for our world conditions today?

The struggle for independence from colonial domination that raged in diverse parts of the world in the twentieth century resulted in the creation of various alliances by the oppressed people to fight for their freedoms. For these oppressed people the objective, which was mainly focused on liberation was clear, and the enemy in most cases seen as the European was well defined. Such alliances between Africans and Asians produced the Afro-Asian and the Arab League groupings, which formed the basis for co-operation and development in both cases.

The 1955 Bandung conference held in Indonesia was the first large scale meeting between emerging independent African[19] and Asian states, and the declared aims of the conference were to oppose colonialism or neocolonialism by any nation and promote Afro-Asian economic and cultural cooperation. The need to form strong alliances at a time when vulnerable nations felt more protected in banding together produced extraordinary solidarity, such conditions may be said to be a factor underpinning the enormous support demonstrated by China in the building of the Tanzania-Zambia railroad.

The Arab League came into existence in 1945 following the adoption of the 1944 Alexandria Protocol in Egypt, with the aim of being a regional organization of Arab states working together to develop members' economies, resolve disputes and coordinate their

---

[19] The African states represented included Ethiopia, Liberia, Sudan, Egypt and Ghana.

political aims. The idea of Arab nationalism is behind the formation of the organization (Toffolo, 2008). United by the use of Arabic as the common language and implicitly by the Islamic religion, Arab nationalism asserts that the Arabs constitute a single nation and as such it is closely linked to Pan-Arabism, the ideology espousing the unification of all Arabs from North Africa to West Asia. However, when necessary the group is able to solicit support outside its Arab focused ideology in seeking to achieve some of its aims.   For example, through its members in what was formally the OAU, African states were successfully persuaded to sever diplomatic relations with Israel after the October 1973 Arab-Israeli war. But how compatible are the notions of Pan-Arabism and Pan-Africanism as expressed in the two ideologies?

Are there any underlying reticent assumptions that inform the post-colonial relations that the Arabs and Asians project into their associations with Africans south of the Sahara? Mazrui (1975) gives us a hint in his statement concerning Arabs and Black Africans that the relationship between the two has always been largely unequal, with the Arabs usually the givers and the Black Africans (meaning those south of the Sahara) usually the receivers. Similarly, Chan (2013) attempts to offer us a revealing insight into the Chinese approach by which Africa is seen as the younger sibling to be led and protected by China, the older brother, and in return receive the necessary respect and devotion from Africa. In both the Arab and Chinese perspectives, it is not too difficult to detect the subordinate role assigned to Africa. In other words, the inferior connotations assumed in what it means to be African are implicitly woven into the ensuing association. Consequently, the difficulty in discounting the silent but powerful element of belittlement in such partnerships in spite of the fine overt gestures of goodwill become manifest from time to time.

Africans remain to be disregarded and exploited for as long as they continue to make little effort to seriously assert their own reality. Winning freedoms is necessary but not altogether sufficient if Africans are to safeguard and maintain their hard won independence in a world that is likely to remain unstable assuming social, economic and environmental conditions follow future projections. The potential magnitude and damaging consequences for Africa through lack of vigilance cannot be overstated. The emerging shape of African-Oriental relationship in the midst of the pressures for economic advancement by individual countries has to some extent overturned the spirit of cooperation that once seemingly existed. For example, the oil producing Arab countries gave Africans no special considerations during the 1973 oil crisis[20] in return for the support they offered the Arabs at the height of the Arab-Israeli conflict. Similarly, China's current business strategy towards Africa appears to be significantly different from the cooperation with Africans during the early stages of African independence. In short, Africans must deeply appreciate the changes that have occurred in terms of economic competitiveness over the course of the last fifty years. They must adjust to the facts of current realities and the dangers posed by foreign nations regardless of whether they were former colonial powers or nations that have also struggled against oppression and are now seeking economic power not only for themselves but over others. Africans therefore must, at

---

[20] The 1973 oil crisis began when members of the Organization of Arab Petroleum Exporting Countries proclaimed an oil embargo, which targeted nations they perceived to be supporting Israel during the Yom Kippur War.

all cost, be prepared to be self-reliant in order to express the true meaning of the freedom they so fervently fought to win.

PART TWO

BEYOND FREEDOM

Freedom is arguably never free and its significance may be understood in terms of the extent of the persistence and quality of the struggle that is conducted for its preservation. The desire for freedom that has been the driving force for independence in Africa also unleashed the unforgiving realities in keeping such hard won freedom. How are Africans managing the challenge of living free after gaining their independence?

CHAPTER FOUR

DEVELOPMENT

How do we explain the lack of development of social and economic wellbeing widespread in Africa? How do we account for the development patterns of some of the leading states that can be considered as symbols of African liberation? Ethiopia having maintained her standing as the oldest African sovereign power remains the symbol of African independence; Haiti, home of the world's only successful revolutionary uprising against slavery to become a republic over two hundred years ago symbolising the tenacity of the African spirit to survive, and Liberia, the first republic on the African mainland led by free slaves and their descendants from the Americas inspired Africans under colonial domination to seek their liberation.

If we consider the proposal by Sen (2000) that we view development as freedom, in other words, as a process of expanding real freedoms that people enjoy rather than simply in terms of the rise in personal income or growth of a nation's gross national product (GDP) then the African world is yet to enjoy such development. For Sen, development as freedom necessitates the removal of the chief sources that inhibit freedom such as poverty, poor economic opportunities as well as facilities for education and health care, neglect of public facilities as well as denial of political and civil rights. Sen not only provides a means of rejuvenating the debate in relation to African development but a powerful perspective for a focused understanding of our world in which, Keita (2011) locates the issues as emanating from the usurpation of the modern state by secular governments locked on to concentrated capital that protect their dominance by two critical methods; the first is by legal self-serving statutes and the second by security systems that often operate in secrecy and with impunity, a system of governmental structure that has been widely adopted in post-colonial Africa.

Democratic Facilities

While it is true that political freedom has come to African states on the mainland and in some parts of the Diaspora, the democratic freedoms that the people should enjoy remain in many ways highly elusive across the African world. For example, some commentators have described Ghana as a beacon of hope (Sithole, 2012) for the African continent chiefly on account of the smooth and peaceful transitions of political power from one administration to the next at various general elections since the early 1990's. While there may be some facts to support this position should Ghanaians become complacent with what they now have as a consolidated democracy?

It is true that Ghanaians now enjoy quite a large number of media outlets comprising of radio and television stations, newspapers and some vibrant civil society organisations and consequently can claim some degree of democratic freedom for society at large. Let it be granted that the roles these institutions assume as custodians of democracy are important, but how objective can these institutions be when they are in some cases manipulated by political party chiefs?

Currently, political parties in Ghana continue to struggle against the pull of ethnicity and thus the potential risk of major electoral violence beyond the low level clashes that occasionally occur during elections remains a conceivable threat, even more so as political power is increasingly viewed as a gateway to uninhibited party and individual material enrichment. This political culture fuelled by the 'winner takes all' mentality is painfully similar across several African states, which, in some cases such as Kenya, Zimbabwe, Cote d'Ivoire and Congo have led to large-scale violence.

The abuse of power by political actors across a number of African states contributed significantly to the litany of open armed conflicts that dominated civil life in considerable parts of Africa over the past decades, continuing into the present century. The future hazard that is likely to unfold in Africa if prevailing conditions remain the same is that of a crippling disorder created by political agents through which limited transparency and responsibility of governments fuel covert lawlessness, greed, corruption and ultimately, the denial of genuine democratic freedoms.

If the kind of seeming democratic instability that Ghana has been spared in recent decades is the basis for it to be viewed as an inspiration for the rest of Africa, then the question that remains to be fully answered is what sort of development does it encourage? Although some points have already been raised earlier, further exploration of this critical question is useful. Underpinning the praise for Ghana as indicated earlier is the relative peacefulness that has apparently become the hallmark of the transitions of power since the 1990's amidst the protests and accusations of vote rigging and foul play that have so far followed each of the elections. The 2012 elections produced a disputed result that terminated in a court case and a near national crisis. Consequently, this incident has opened up a new stage in the Ghanaian political process as it unlocks the possibility for the courts to come to decide winners and losers of future elections in spite of electoral commissions and the results they endorse.

The current Ghanaian political system faces potential future problems on a number of issues. Firstly, the present four-year electoral cycle places time limitations on what presiding governments can realistically accomplish before the next election. For example, a newly elected government may sensibly spend its first year seeking and appointing its key members to important positions, then the second year may be used to attempt to implement its manifesto and by the third year the gathering heat of the impending election is very likely to begin to distract and distort the focus of the government as it enters and faces its final year in power and an election to contest. Secondly, this situation as described above places untold pressures on political parties and individual politicians to do all they possibly can to preserve their positions if they happen to be in the ruling party, and similarly for those in the opposition parties to use any appropriate means imaginable to satisfy their intense craving for access to power. As a result, the tension between the weak but supposedly growing nature of the democratic processes on the one hand, and the 'winner takes all' attitude that has become firmly embedded in the Ghanaian body politic on the other hand, exacerbate the delicate balance as the seductiveness of the latter continues to reinforce all kinds of shenanigans for gaining political power and personal riches over the shortest period of time.

Is it possible for Ghana to plan and successfully implement very long term development plans in tandem with the short-termism that is at the heart of its political system? The constitution as it stands for example, continues to suffer from some provisions such as the indemnity clauses that fundamentally conflict with the democratic tenets of probity, accountability and equity for all. While it can be argued that such indemnity provisions are the price for Ghana's democratic stability, the question that this raises is what kind of democracy does it encourage? Such conditions only stand to mock the genuine adherence to vital democratic principles. In other words, the inbuilt mixed messages forced onto the constitution if not addressed, may in the long term contribute to undermining the credibility of the democratic system in practice. As already indicated, Ghana's elevation to the status of a 'beacon of hope' for Africa by some commentators is heavily predicated on the apparent peaceful transitions of power, which should be applauded. However, the increasing complexities of political issues that accompany each election cast a dangerous shadow over the future development of the democratic process in Ghana and as such it is reasonable to assign the judgement of the durability of Ghana's political progress to future generations.

While the huge financial resources committed by politicians and political parties to contesting multi party elections make up the norm in democratic systems the world over, the weak institutional structures such as the civil service and the judiciary that currently exist to keep such as practices appropriately regulated in Africa implies that corruption, rigging of election results and the accumulation of dishonest wealth by various politicians aided by their lackeys and some state officials go unchecked. These prevailing issues present an unfortunate situation that can easily contribute to the distortion of the fundamental institutional arrangements required for controlling such malpractices as a prerequisite for promoting desirable democratic values.

The modern state in Africa is a result of an inherited colonial system that the African ruling elites have so far been unable to transform into an all inclusive system of government, and have mainly succeeded in entrenching their own interests by exploiting various elements such as ethnicity, religion and patrimonial politics. The overall effect has been a failure to provide the needed democratic facilities such as freedom of speech and assembly, quality education and health services, basic access to clean water and efficient system of sanitation for its citizenry to thrive. Political power in the growing patrimonial and plunder-focused politics in Africa is not concentrated in a political environment, but often in one individual who applies it for their self-interest in ways that loyal supporters are selectively favoured and rewarded with little room for dissenting voices, which unsurprisingly lead to the co-opting or suppressing of popular leaders. This condition is very likely to be a major contributing factor underpinning not only the chaotic nature of African elections and politics but also the general lack of provision of social opportunities for Africans.

Social Opportunities

What in some sense could be observed as a paradox is that Africa holds a large proportion of the world's natural resources and yet it ranks among the most poverty stricken and desolate realms. Although numerous reasons have been given by commentators concerning why Africa remains poor[21], clear or convincing explanations are yet to be put forward by African leaders to justify their situation after more than half a century of independence across most of Africa. What advancements have African states made since gaining their sovereignty? What provisions have African leaders successfully and sustainably made for the enhancement of social opportunities for the African people?

Let us grant that the commentaries on Africa have not been all strictly gloomy[22], however, while numerous observers (Mahajan, 2009; Robertson, 2012; World Economic and Financial Surveys, 2011 & 2014) have made positive comments regarding the growth opportunities open to Africa, many of the observations and comments focus on future possibilities. Similarly, a recent special report in the Financial Times highlighted the rise in per capita in African gross domestic product being enjoyed by the continent as a result of robust economic growth unparalleled since the decolonisation period of the 1960's and 1970's:

> A virtuous circle of healthy growth in the continent's economies – supported by high commodity prices and

---

[21] For example see Walter Rodney (1988) on How Europe Underdeveloped Africa.

[22] The Economist published on 3rd Dec 2011 first carried the report on Africa Rising

cheap Chinese loans – and improved governance have led to a new chapter that many call "Africa Rising".

By and large, the military remain in their barracks: democracy, even if imperfect, has spread through the continent and has seen the rise of an increasingly powerful independent media.

The new dawn has lifted Africa's profile, attracting billions of dollars in foreign investment. With a pool of young talent, fertile land and abundant commodities, many hope that Africa could, at the very least, play a larger role in global business.

Still, the journey to fulfill those hopes remains tortuous: corruption remains rampant and governments are doing very little to build institutions for the long term. The media are under attack in many countries and some politicians are trying every trick in the book to extend their mandate beyond the legal term.

Economic growth, even if robust, remains unequal, with poverty and unemployment on the rise.

(Financial Times, 5th October 2014)

Considering the persistence and growth in poverty and unemployment in spite of the boom in Africa some commentators have expressed misgivings concerning the familiar narrative of a booming continent. Jerven (2013) takes particular issue with the deficiency inherent in statistical capacity at the heart of measuring African wealth and progress. The argument is that the arbitrariness of the quantification process produces observations with large errors and levels of uncertainty, and the potentially misleading air of accuracy that the resulting numbers assume go into making critical decisions that ultimately allocate scares resources. While it is important to note that issues regarding the validity of statistical components are not problems uniquely restricted to Africa, what is of deep concern is the primacy and impact of such inaccuracies in the judgements that international development agencies make based on erroneous statistics. Similarly, governments are unable to make informed decisions because existing data needed are too weak or do not simply exist. In short, poor statistical numbers fundamentally shape what is known about development in Africa, which in turn structures how decisions are made. Jervan cautions that the most basic matric of development, which is GDP[23] should not be treated as an objective number but instead as a number that is a product of a process in which a range of random and contentious assumptions are made. In other words, 'the metric should be used with the utmost care' since the quality of the number is reliant on the quality of the system that produces the statistics and unfortunately, in many poor countries of which Africa has a large number, these systems are deficient. The situation in some way illuminates some of the potential confusion surrounding reports on Africa's economic 'rise' and its adequacy in reflecting reality.

Ghana, which is often cited as one of the fastest growing economies in Africa and set to benefit from a relatively recent oil discovery, the reality of so called middle class life in the country differs from the experiences of those in other parts of the world. Basic amenities such as water, electricity and gas are yet to be made adequately and constantly available as the nation continues to struggle with shortages. Meanwhile the growing gap between the rich and poor suggests that the living conditions of the less fortunate struggling to survive may be deteriorating. In spite of a decade of apparently high growth across the African continent, the wealth being created does not seem to be equally shared, resulting in the limited progress in its human

---

[23] Gross Domestic Product

development[24]. The evidence clearly suggests that the current growth is not just a case of the rich getting richer but this is happening at the expense of the poor who are getting poorer.

For a large section of the growing population in Africa, the limited availability of quality healthcare and education present serious challenges. A recent report[25] by the Economist Intelligence Unit (EIU) contends that as in other parts of the world, Africa must reexamine its healthcare systems to ensure that they are viable over the next decade. However, what makes this exceptionally difficult is that it must do so while dealing with a broad range of healthcare, political and economic difficulties. In addition to having some of the most impoverished populations in the world, the continent is facing various epidemiological crises concurrently. High levels of communicable and parasitic disease such as malaria, tuberculosis, and above all HIV/AIDS are being matched by growing rates of chronic conditions. While the communicable diseases are the best known, it is the chronic conditions such as heart disease that are looming as the greater future threat.

Furthermore, continued high rates of maternal and child mortality exert further burden on a system that is already inadequate for the challenges facing it. The EIU report also noted that healthcare delivery organization in Africa is simply insufficient and skilled healthcare workers together with crucial medicines are in less than adequate supply. Consequently, the inefficiency inherent in the procurement and distribution systems is leading

---

[24] Report in The Guardian Newspaper 24th February 2014.
[25] See http://www.janssen-emea.com/sites/default/files/The%20Future%20of%20Healthcare%20in%20Africa.pdf

to unequal access to treatment. Due to insufficient public spending on health the poorest Africans have little or no access to care. In addition, the poor also frequently lack access to the very basic prerequisites of health such as clean water, sanitation and adequate nutrition. The issue regarding sanitation is particularly disturbing as a study on the state of sanitation in Africa (Morella et al, 2008) suggest that nearly all the states in Sub-Saharan Africa are likely to miss the Millennium Development Goal for access to improved sanitation. Though sanitation has not been directly linked to the emergence of the devastating Ebola virus in parts of West Africa that caused panic across the globe, it may possibly assist to propel the dreadful sanitation problem as a critical factor to tackle. Considering the huge challenges facing Africa's healthcare systems, numerous major improvements will be needed across the continent to ensure their sustainability in the long term. An important aspect in keeping people healthy is by shifting the focus of healthcare from curing to preventative care and undoubtedly, education is a critical element in doing so.

In spite of the worldwide positive trends on general progress in educational provision and fulfilments Africa nevertheless presents some causes for long-term concerns. According to an IMF report[26], primary enrolment and school completion rates in sub-Saharan Africa show meaningful progress in line with developments in other developing countries elsewhere, however, the improvement in Africa's human development index is lagging relative to the corresponding improvement worldwide. Consequently,

---

[26] Regional economic outlook: Sub-Saharan Africa- Fostering Durable and Inclusive Growth. See
https://www.imf.org/external/pubs/ft/reo/2014/afr/eng/sreo0414.htm

progress in archiving the Millennium goals has been uneven and slower than needed to reach the 2015 target. Africa faces a twin crisis of access to education and quality of learning, according to a new research mechanism[27]. This first region-wide survey of learning on the continent covering 28 sub-Saharan nations estimates that a third of children of primary school age will reach their adolescent years unable to read, write or perform basic numeracy tasks, and in addition, the number of out of school children is set to increase in the foreseeable future. Estimates by the United Nations (Smith, 2013) indicate that the world needs 8 million more teachers by 2015 in order to achieve its Millennium Goal for education and of these, 6 million are required to replace others who will leave the teaching profession, while 2 million are necessary extra teachers. And more than half of those necessary extra teachers are needed in Sub-Saharan Africa.

Considering that literacy and numeracy are needed as functional skills for modern societies, access to the world and satisfaction, basic tools for individual advancement, and a personal source of knowledge, all of which, if we apply Sen's conception of development then the challenge for Africa remains very steep. The importance of the quality of the relevant social facilities including human resources to aid African development cannot be overemphasised as it is at the heart of any serious considerations for core societal advancement.

---

[27] The Africa Learning Barometer is an interactive feature that analyzes the state of education and learning in sub-Saharan Africa. It is collaboration between the Brookings Center for Universal Education and the *Financial Times*. See https://www.brookings.edu/interactives/africa-learning-barometer/

Human Capital

The natural resource richness of the African continent is clearly undeniable and yet Africa is among the least developed areas in the world. Centuries of disruptions in the existence and advancement of Africans by external forces and its perpetuation by internal African elements are in many ways serious contributing factors to the continent's stunted development.   The continuing movement of Africans en masse as a result of various catastrophes, or as economic migrants in search of better opportunities elsewhere, or as gifted individuals seeking outlets for their talents, underscore the depth of the problem and the need for enduring solutions.

The significance of human resources in the life and progress of any nation is too obvious to clarify and consequently its constant improvement is essential. For Africa to improve on its development it has to include among its major focuses the development of its people, a point well captured in the following World Bank report (2000) statement:

> Africa's future lies in its people. Indeed, Africa must solve its current human development crisis if it is to claim the 21st century... Investment in people is becoming more important for two reasons. First, Africa's future economic growth will depend less on its natural resources, which are being depleted and are subject to long-run price declines and more on its labour skills and its ability to accelerate a demographic transition. Growth in today's information-based world economy depends on a flexible, educated, and healthy workforce to take advantage of economic openness (p.103).

The criticality of people in the production of knowledge, goods and services is an obvious and important consideration that African nations stand to benefit if they commit to investing thoroughly in it.

Education as already indicated is one of the key elements in the development of human resource in Africa. However, some major challenges facing most African nations in expanding their educational provision (Pillay, 2005) include limited resources in terms of national spending per student; inequality due to the rich within society capturing a larger portion than the poor; inefficiency as a result of lack of teaching materials and low-quality teaching, which together impact on the quality of learning. In spite of the debilitating conditions under which most African children experience teaching and learning, the talented within the population continue to find avenues to express their talents. Unfortunately, the search for opportunities to develop and improve result in the exodus of young bright Africans to foreign lands in what has long been recognised and studied as 'brain drain'.

A study of human movement and its impact on development in Africa (Tanner, 2005) provided some interesting perspectives and proposed some means by which some of the issues that it raises may be tackled. The movement of people from one place to another is a phenomenon that occurs across the globe and is often triggered by a number of critical factors such as human conflicts, natural disasters, economic conditions, individual preferences, etc. Thus the movement of Africans within the global context can be considered as no different from those occurring elsewhere. However, what is deeply worrying is the form and impact of such movements on the African communities. For example, the current migration out of Africa is made up of predominantly young men and women who should under normal circumstances be contributing the bulk of the labour for African development.

Brain drain as a result of the migration of highly skilled or talented Africans from their communities to centres of comparatively higher financial and other rewards as perceived to be the case in the Western world is an example. There are some positive benefits of international labour migration, for example, the receiving country may benefit from the productivity of the talented migrant and in the context of a friendly destination country the wellbeing of the individual is likely to increase as this is facilitated through better educational and career opportunities, higher salaries and possible higher standards of living. Furthermore this increase in wellbeing may also result in some positive impact in the individual's country of origin through remittances and the creation of business related opportunities. For example, a recent report (Ehrhart et al, 2014) suggests that migrants foster what may amount to significant contributions to exports in Africa. However, the dangers posed by excessive emigration to African nations if it is not sensibly managed cannot be ignored. In the long term, a brain drain's decreasing effect can only be achieved by a carefully planned and effective means of combating poverty. But to achieve this goal, it is clear that in addition to, and beyond the foreign aid that African governments receive, this can ultimately be reached through independent development by African states. To simply be reliant on aid and remittances African states can only be considered as economic failure.

As already discussed, while much has been reported about Africa rising and the possible good times ahead, it still remains to be fully explained why the youth of

Africa continue to breach Europe's border fences whenever they can in the attempt to gain entry, and where this is not possible, to risk their lives and in many cases drown trying to cross the Mediterranean sea to Europe in any floatable structure? What are the possible causes driving the youth out of Africa? Lack of meaningful employment must feature prominently among the many possible reasons that can be given. Furthermore, underpinning the lack of employment is the issue of poor educational experience that most have gained, a condition that can only exacerbate the continuing wastage of talent. Africa must not merely continue to depend on the extraction of its natural resources as the main source of income but must uncompromisingly harness its human capital for use in the production of goods and services and better ways of living. Failing to grasp the opportunity to do so will not only condemn generations to living unfulfilling and degrading lives, but also lead to the ultimate deterioration of Africa. Moreover, the expected growth in population over the foreseeable future together with the uncertain impact of impending environmental issues are additional potential problems and these issues will be the focus of our discussions in the next chapter.

CHAPTER FIVE

ENVIRONMENTAL ISSUES

The upheavals that affect us in diverse ways in our world such as the periodic political and economic chaos may not be the only challenges that we will encounter in the future. Environmental challenges are set to impact on the human population in ways that are yet to be understood. For example, the rising level of the sea as a result of environmental changes is most probably set to threaten islands and communities inhabiting lowlands and areas below sea level on our planet. Data collection in addition to unfolding situations point to our need to adequately plan to meet the probable changes ahead. However, the situation in Africa is raising serious cause for concern as on-going studies suggest extreme experiences to occur in Africa, meanwhile African governments and institutions are yet to make concerted efforts in preparation for the perceived changes to come.

The Unfolding Situation

New studies highlighted in a newspaper report[28] suggest that a major factor in the popular uprisings across North

---

[28] The Observer report 'Climate change: how a warming world is a threat to our food supplies.' 13th April 2013.

Africa, which became known as the Arab Spring was related to food insecurity. Droughts, food and water shortages and a combination of other environmental factors are predicted to exacerbate political tensions in Africa and as such, the urgent need for planning and preparation as food prices spiral and long standing agricultural practices are disrupted by climate change need no justification. There is much alarm and controversy in the claim[29] that Africa is poised to experience a surge in civil wars, which may cause nearly 400,000 additional battle deaths by 2030 and all as a direct result of rising temperatures and its impact on reduced crop yields or other aspects of economic productivity which, will inevitably lead to the increase in social tension. But how are we to understand the nature of the changes taking place?

Conway (2009), an eminent scientist on climate change argues that the African climate is determined at the macro-level by three major drivers namely, tropical convection, the alternating of the monsoons, and the El Niño-Southern Oscillation of the Pacific Ocean. According to Conway, the first two are local processes that determine the regional and seasonal patterns of temperature and rainfall, however the third is more remote in its origin, but strongly influences the year-to-year rainfall and temperature patterns in Africa. Conway admits that our understanding of how these drivers interact and are affected by climate change is insufficient and in need of improvement, but maintains that over the next 100 years the drier subtropical regions will warm more than the moister tropics. Northern and Southern Africa will become much hotter and drier. Wheat production in the north and maize

---

[29] New Scientist Magazine 'African conflict spurred by warming.' 23rd November 2009.

production in the south are likely to be adversely affected. In Eastern Africa, including the horn of Africa, and parts of Central Africa average rainfall is likely to increase. A worrying estimation is the likelihood of the spread and severity of vector borne diseases such as malaria and dengue fever and furthermore, in the next fifty years the sea levels will rise, with serious consequences in the Nile delta and certain parts of West Africa. While there is much that we are yet to know concerning the magnitudes of the impending disruptions, a careful attention to the probable impacts of climate change may help us to start planning best possible responses to the unfolding situation.

The expected rise in sea levels around the globe as a result of global warming has, as its primary cause, the thermal expansion of the oceans due to the rising oceanic temperatures. However, this prediction is dependent on various factors including the melting rate of the Greenland ice sheet within the Arctic Circle. According to Conway (2009) Africa however, is less likely to be as damaged by rising sea level nevertheless a one metre rise in the sea level say, could cause extensive damage in the Nile Delta. Similarly, there are likely to be severe impacts along the West coast of Africa. For example the capital of Gambia, Banjul is likely to be submerged in the future. In Ghana, a relatively small rise in sea level could have seriously damaging consequences precipitated by increased coastal erosion (Addo et al, 2011), leading to the destruction of wetlands and associated industries and more crucially in the accelerated loss of some areas of Accra, the capital of Ghana. Based on these projections therefore, say a six metre rise in sea levels as a result of a more rapid than expected acceleration in the melting of one or both the

Arctic and Antarctic ice caps could have even more catastrophic consequences.

The heavy flooding of parts of both western and eastern Africa in 2007 provide some indication of the higher frequency of more intense downpours to come even in the drier regions. The congregation of direct and indirect results of flooding can only exacerbate the difficulties that Africans face with regard to their wellbeing. It is ironical that while flooding is expected to increase, so too is drought predicted to rise both in the short and long term with similar consequences of loss of lives, damage to crops and livestock and so on. The inter-relatedness of the impact of drought on agricultural production and food security as a result of climatic change is particularly worrying as prolonged high temperatures and periods of drought will inevitably force large regions of marginal agricultural engagement out of production.

Water scarcity as a threat to livelihood in Africa is emerging as a source of major difficulty. As the population in Africa is expected to increase over the coming decades and becoming increasingly urban means that demand for water as a consequence is very likely to create serious challenges in the near future. It is very likely that over the next few decades Africa's population may double. With a current growth rate of over 3% per year (Smith, 2013) the population is very likely to maintain the fastest growth rate in the world. The forecast[30] is that by 2030, almost 50% of Africa's population will become urban dwellers. Naturally, demand for water as a consequence of population growth in cities in combination with industrial requirements on one hand, and its demand for

---

[30] See KPMG report on 'The role of cities in Africa's rise' (2012)

agriculture and power on the other hand is very likely to put unbearable pressure on the decreasing water recourses available. As demand for water grows, cities will be forced to rely on water sources from further away risking deterioration in water quality as it becomes more expensive to tap.

The direct effect of high temperature on human health is yet another potential impact of climate change as rising temperatures can result in loss of life. However, other health consequences are likely to be borne indirectly through diseases carried by insects and other vectors that are sensitive to the effects of changing temperatures. For example, small changes in temperature can boost the population of disease-carrying mosquitoes, which may result in the increase in malaria epidemics (Lindsay and Martens, 1998).

The impact of climate change on Africa's biodiversity is simply incalculable. Given the heavy dependence on natural resources in Africa, many communities are seriously vulnerable to the biodiversity loss that may result. Africa indeed comprises a wide variety of ecosystems including savannahs and tropical forests, coral reefs and major inland waters and together, Africa occupies about one-fifth of the global land surface and contains about one-fifth of all known species of plants, mammals, and birds in the world, as well as one-sixth of amphibians and reptiles (Siegfried, 1989). As a result of the impending climate change it has been suggested (Thomas, et al, 2004) that globally, approximately 15% to 40% of land plants and animal species will become extinct by 2050. The delicate ecosystems of dry and semi-humid lands are particularly vulnerable as small changes in temperature can result in detrimental effects on the sustainability of plants and animals.

Changes in a variety of ecosystems (Boko, et al, 2007) are already occurring particularly in the southern African ecosystems, at a faster rate than anticipated. Furthermore, climate change in association with human drivers such as deforestation constitutes a threat to Africa's forest ecosystem. For example, in the Sahel region of Western Africa, which is vulnerable to climate hazards, an assessment of the impact on important crops such as sorghum yields (Sultan, et al, 2014) indicated future decreases in mean crop yields and increases in year-to-year vulnerability of crop yields in the Western part of the Sahel. Animal biodiversity on the African continent is also concentrated in these regions and any loss or alterations to these habitats by climate change in addition to increasing competition with humans is very likely to have disastrous impact. Similarly, marine ecosystems are also very likely to suffer adversely.

As indicated earlier, a broad scientific and political consensus has been established that climate change poses a grave and alarming threat to Africa, its ecosystems and its diverse species including the human population. The world's poorest communities with the majority living in Africa are more likely to suffer disproportionately the consequences of climate change. The poor in Africa for example, already bear the heavy burden of pollution, degradation of natural resources and land. In light of these growing concerns how is Africa in particular preparing for the future with projected changes of such magnitudes in our global climatic conditions?

The Necessary Preparation

Much attention has been drawn to the view that Africa is one of the most vulnerable continents to climate change, a situation being provoked by the interaction of multiple factors occurring at various levels including the geographical position of the continent. The current estimation for the future is severe due to the considerably limited capacity for mitigation and adaptation, which is furthermore exacerbated by the widespread poverty and the lack of development.

In spite of the growing knowledge and confidence concerning climate change and its possible effects on the planet, much more remains unknown in relation to Africa. Many questions remain to be answered such as: Will the flow of the Nile increase or decrease? Will the total fall in agricultural production be very large or relatively small? Will the Sahel Belt get wetter or remain dry? Conway (2009) argues that part of our ignorance in answering such questions comes from our poor understanding of the drivers of the African climate and their complex interactions, and part is due to a severe lack of local weather data. Consequently, this lack of knowledge makes it problematic to verify climatic models and therefore predict with any degree of confidence what will occur as a result of changes in the climate at a country or sub-regional level in Africa. Two major implications surface as a result of our relatively poor state of knowledge. The first is the need for urgent research into both the dynamics of the global drivers and the detailed consequences at local levels. The second is the need to design adaptation measures to cope with the high levels of uncertainty. The question to be considered at this point is this: how seriously are Africans taking the looming threat posed by climate change and preparing for it? In order to consider this question let us first ascertain some of the key elements involved.

As already discussed above, the assumption is that numerous regions of Africa will suffer from droughts and floods with greater frequency and intensity therefore adaptation will depend on developing resilience through the uncertain times ahead. The notion of resilience being considered is comparable to how natural disasters such as earthquakes, floods, bushfires and tsunamis have been endured in the past. The process begins with the forecasting of the likely disaster then proceeds to developing preventative and tolerance measures that focus on recovery and restoration after the occurrence of the event (Conway, 2009). Moreover this method becomes more proactive than reactive as it is inserted, where possible, in the routine risk management and then appraised at various stages in terms of the relevant criteria including the associated costs and benefits. However learning remains crucial throughout the process and therefore it is prudent for more time and resources to be committed in the earlier and sustainable stages of the process.

Given the above background context we can now focus on the preparations that Africans are making in anticipation of the unfolding situation. It is true that the impact of climatic change is not entirely new in Africa as a sizable portion of the population is familiar with natural disasters. But the crucial point is how well they are preparing to cope with the possible changes in the scale and nature of the impact as the pace of climate change increases. Clearly, in order to begin to respond positively to the changes that are already occurring greater investment in adaptation is needed now.

Unfortunately, majority of African states rank among the least prepared for the impending climate change according to recent data released in 2014 by Global Adaptation Index[31].

What are some of the issues hindering African nations from developing effective systems in anticipation of the impending climatic changes? African states have been engaged in climate change discussions through the African Union and even developed what became known as the African common position as the basis for negotiating favourable terms for Africa. However, the confusing positions signalled by the Africans to the international community weakened their position, which eventually ended the negotiation strategy of the African common position. Consequently the united front they initially presented gave way to concessions made through internal strife[32], once again demonstrating the tragic inability of Africans to confront their common problems in unity. The issue of lack of African unity which we will discuss more fully later, remains a serious problem as it presents a stumbling block in Africa's development and in this particular case how they collaborate to face the uncertain future that climate change, a phenomenon that has no meaning in terms of political or geographical borders.

---

[31] This is the world's leading annual index that ranks nearly two hundred countries based on their vulnerability to climate change and their preparedness to adapt to the natural disasters that climate change can trigger. It is a project based at the University of Notre Dame. See www.index.gain.org
[32] See Hoste, Jean-Christophe 2010: Where was united Africa in the climate change negotiations? European Development Cooperation to 2020. http://www.edc2020.eu/fileadmin/Textdateien/post_COP_15_briefing/Jean_Christophe_Hoste_-_Where_was_united_Africa_in_the_climate_change_negotiations_-_EDC_2020.pdf

The African Union (AU) speaks on behalf of Africa in negotiations concerning climate change. In the AU's declaration on Climate Change and Development in Africa, leaders of member states acknowledged the continent's economic and production systems' vulnerability to climate change and stressed that climate change could endanger future wellbeing of the population, ecosystems and socio-economic progress of the continent. Furthermore, they pledged to promote the application of science and technology for climate data collection, analysis and generation of early warning information system. Since these declarations and commitments were made in 2007 it is still difficult to obtain a clear idea of the progress made in bringing them to fruition.

It is true that Africa has contributed negligibly to greenhouse gas emissions however, it must be said that this is not due to making the right choices but precisely because of Africa's lack of industrial structures to reach worrying levels of emissions. It could be argued that the tendencies of numerous industrial development plans in Africa also subscribe to the powerful competitiveness and growth models underpinning much of the industrial activities of the developed world which Africa is eager to hold accountable for polluting the atmosphere and seeking to extract some form of compensation.

While greenhouse gases may be seen as crucial in climate change other factors such as deforestation through logging of hectares of forests can also contribute to climate variation and ultimately to disastrous impacts on humans. Equally, pollution of rivers by industrial and municipal waste and damming of rivers do contribute to damaging the environment and livelihoods. For example, the chemical and solid waste pollution of the Congo River is a cause for concern[33]. Similarly, the environmental impacts of dams highlight the need for extensive reconsideration by African states yearning for industrialization by means of damming some of the rivers in Africa. The River Nile for example, currently supports numerous dams and possibly more planned for the future. This situation eventually could seriously contribute to long-term negative impacts on the environment and communities living along the Nile. The consequences of building large dams[34] are numerous and varied, contributing negatively to the biological, chemical and physical properties of rivers and riparian environments. Dams prevent fish migrations and trap sediments that are essential for maintaining habitats and productive deltas, wetlands, fertile floodplains and so on further downstream thereby keeping the entire river system alive. A clear and important impact is the artificial lake that free flowing river ecosystems are forced to become upstream, thus changing the essential character of the rivers as the constant evolution of life in and around these rivers are conditioned on the timings of the ebbs and flows. In addition to their environmental impacts, dams also have severe economic and social impacts. According to a report on large dams produced by the World Commission on Dams (Dams, 2000), on average such dams have been at best only marginally economically viable and have forced between 40-80 million people from their lands over the past seven decades. The Volta dam in Ghana is an interesting case as its current viability has increasingly become

---

[33] See the executive summary at
http://www.unep.org/dewa/giwa/areas/reports/r42/executive_summary_giwa_r42.pdf
[34] View info at http://www.internationalrivers.org/environmental-impacts-of-dams

questionable having displaced communities for its construction.

The building of large dams continues to hold sway as the model for development and consequently present issues that Africans must take into account in seeking feasible sustainable solutions not solely on national basis but also towards adopting and implementing unified practical approaches across Africa, a strategic method that we will later examine further. Ultimately, Africans can find collective solutions to the unfolding environmental issues if they can overcome the challenge inherent in the difficulties they have working together for a common goal. If African states fail to find ways to achieve their common goals then the prospect of future conflict may be intensified as resources deplete. Salient recommendations including the need for AU member states to work together on adaptation and mitigation technology and for the AU as an organization to commit to the development of a comprehensive response to climate change have been offered (van Wyk, 2010) toward the improvement, enhancement and sustainment of the AU's response to climate security.

What can we deduce from their climate change negotiations as exemplified in the conflicting needs and interests of AU member states? Could it be that one reason for Africa's ambivalence and inability to commit to a clear, inclusive group approach concerning climate change is due to the complexity inherent in their yearning to industrialize but pursuing such goals by the models and methods of the developed world that is now no longer tenable or sustainable? Could Africa use climate change as an opportunity to become a leader in sustainable development?

Sustainable Living

The urgency concerning how we combat climate change has become sharper over the decades as changes to some glacial formations in the arctic regions for example, intensify.

The rising environmental issues facing mankind today can no longer be ignored. Orr (1992) summarised our contribution to the problem some decades ago as follows:

> If today is a typical day on planet earth, humans will add fifteen million tons of carbon to the atmosphere, destroy 115 square miles of tropical rainforest, create seventy-two square miles of desert, eliminate between forty to one hundred species, erode seventy-one million tons of topsoil and twenty-seven hundred tons of CFCs to the stratosphere, and increase their population by 263,000 (p3).

After two decades and more how do we assess the situation emphasized by Orr? Clearly, if this process is allowed to continue uninterrupted then a global catastrophe is conceivable in the not so distant future. But on what basis does Orr make his observation? It could be argued that the current environmental issues with particular reference to the changes in climatic conditions form part of a natural planetary cycle. Further attention will later be drawn to this view. One likely basis for Orr's argument is the Brundlandt Report, entitled *Our Common Future,* in which the findings of the World Commission on Environment and Development (WCED, 2009) were presented.

The report essentially articulated the numerous problems around the world. It stressed the critical and globally threatening environmental problems, which are now emerging as a result of both the poverty in the South and excessive consumption in the North. It introduced issues of intra- and inter-generational equity, and argued that the increasingly alarming and unsustainable consequences of development on the environment could not be addressed without considerable international co-operation. The report maintained that the future wellbeing of the North was not only dependent upon changing its development trajectory towards more sustainable practices, but would fail unless countries of the South were also prepared to make important adjustments. The report emphasized its belief in humanity's ability to make development sustainable and called for a new era of sensible global economic development and growth in a way that addresses the planet's ecological limits and at the same time meets the legitimate desires and needs of people. It introduced the now well-known notion of 'sustainable development'; defining it as:

> ...development that meets the needs of the present without compromising the ability of future generations to meet their own needs (p43).

The idea of sustainable development does imply some limitations imposed by the present state of technology and social organization on environmental resources and by the ability of the biosphere to absorb the effects of human activities. However, the report concluded that technology and social organization could be both managed and improved to make way for a new era of economic growth.

The need for some kind of transformation in our human lifestyles as a result of the unfolding conditions relating to climate change offers Africa a unique opportunity in assuming a leading role. The motivation for Africans to do so can be easily linked to two reasons, the first is the expectation that the continent is very likely to experience some of the worst outcomes of climate change, and the second is based on the fact that Africa has not yet developed industrial structures comparable to those in the developed world. This suggests that seeking alternative means to developing sustainably may be challenging but can be more boldly initiated as there are no entrenched industrial patterns of behaviour to overcome. In relation to the first reason, we need not labour much in establishing the case as we have already highlighted some of the attendant issues in our earlier discussions that are predicted to affect much of the Sub-Saharan region of the continent. However, the second reason requires some further exploration.

The first industrial revolution that began in Great Britain and was then propagated throughout Western Europe and North America resulted in the transition to new manufacturing processes from about the mid eighteenth century. Deane (1965) summed it up that the route to affluence lies by way of an industrial revolution, and went on to define this as:

> A continuous – some would say self-sustaining – process of economic growth, whereby (wars and natural disasters apart) each generation can confidently expect to enjoy higher levels of production and consumption than its predecessors, is open only to those nations which industrialize (p1).

Consequently, the disparity between the standards of living of the inhabitants of the advanced countries and the standards prevailing in the underdeveloped countries, argues Deane, is essentially due to the fact that the former have industrialised and the latter have not. For Deane, while there is no definite process or event called an industrial revolution that takes the same form across the countries in which it occurs, there are certain identifiable changes in the methods and characteristics of economic organisation when taken together constitute a development of the kind that can be described as an industrial revolution. These include:

> 1) widespread and systematic application of modern scientific and empirical knowledge to the process of production for the market; 2) specialization of economic activity directed towards production for national and internal markets rather for family or parochial use; 3) movement of population from rural to urban communities; 4) enlargement and depersonalization of the typical unit of production so that it comes to be based less on the family or tribe and more on the corporate or public enterprise; 5) movement of labour from activities concerned with the production of primary products to the production of manufactured goods and services; 6) intensive and extensive use of capital resources as a substitute for and compliment to human effort; 7) emergence of new social and occupational classes determined by ownership of or relationship to the means of production other than land, namely capital. These interrelated changes, if they develop together and to a sufficient degree, constitute an industrial revolution (pp1-2).

From Deane's perspective these changes have always been associated with a growth of population and the increase in the annual volume of goods and services produced. If the factors that characterise industrial development as explained by Deane depend on the expansion of key resources and finished products then the implication for Africa attempting to follow a similar route to future development and prosperity is a monumental challenge.

It is arguable that the immense difficulty for Africa to follow the classical route to development can be located in its lack of certain key factors such as technology and financial resources to name a few. If we view this classical route as consisting of the methods such as access to raw materials, cheap labour, capital, technology and markets that eventually defined the process of industrialisation as employed by the premier industrialised nations in their attainment of such status then the predicament of the African situation is thrown into sharp relief. As an opposing example, one could point to the industrialisation of some Asian countries, let us say Japan, to nullify the case made earlier. It is true that Japan became a super industrialised nation and an economic miracle only a few decades after World War Two. However, it achieved this status with massive American foreign support that was part of the reconstruction process after the devastation caused by the war. Admittedly, Japan, unlike Africa, had a highly skilled pre-war labour force and management structure (Moore, 1993) that it could draw on and put to peaceful use after the war. While the aftermath of the war contributed to the rapid industrialisation process for Japan, the upshot of the African struggle for decolonisation on the other hand did not result in any substantial industrialisation that was hoped for across Africa. In view of this state of affairs Africans however can learn to appreciate their potential position in taking considerable advantage of what sustainable development will have to offer nations in the foreseeable future. In other words, the ability to seek development methods in tune with sustainable living and thus different from that offered by the classical route should be of great assistance to Africa.

And here we come to the crux of the problem. Africa cannot meet the environmental challenge effectively and enduringly in its present state of fragmentation. If so, the question that arises and even cries out for an answer is:

which states or group of states coming together can provide the leadership to take the continent out of the present dead end and the potential future crises? Let us now turn to how Africans can begin to take advantage of their unique position

CHAPTER SIX

OPPORTUNITIES IN DIVERSITY

In these unfolding times of unsettling conditions concerning human existence due to critical issues such as climate change, political instabilities and economic confusions for example, the need for Africans to find ways to cope with these rapid changes is more than ever very desperate. The climatic forecasts and the far-reaching implications predicted for Africa as already mentioned in our earlier discussions can be viewed as an opportunity to galvanise the resolve of Africans to use their diversity as a strength in defining a new understanding and cooperation in tackling the monumental problems facing them. While this may be the most reasonable way forward, formidable obstacles remain to be tackled.

Peace Defying Conditions

The ostensible cultural diversity among African people underpins the perception of the vast number of people who view Africa as anything but a continent of one people. For many the diversity in language, local traditions, long-standing hostilities between some neighbouring communities and the enduring colonial boundaries that have artificially divided communities and families across Africa for the past few centuries provide the evidence for their view of Africa as a divided continent. Let us examine some of these factors that have helped to entrench such views.

The subject of Africa immediately conjures up the word "tribe" for most people around the world and the general connotation associated with the use of the word is primitiveness. Few people question the description of an African community as a "tribe" in news stories describing Africa; indeed many Africans themselves use the word "tribe" when speaking or writing about identity in African states. Some of the most brutal conflicts in Africa were in most cases ignited by the alleged ethnic differences that some Africans have come to hold dear. For example, the so-called tribal allegiances underpinned the Rwandan massacres in 1994, the 2007 Kenyan elections violence and the decades long killings in the Sudan. The persistence of the entrenched perceptions of ethnic differences upon which some Africans are led to commit violence and murder against other Africans is a tragic situation that seem to have no easy solution. What are some of the underlying reasons for the antagonistic feelings between some African communities?

In spite of the widespread assumption that tribalism is a remnant of traditional pre-colonial Africa reflecting ancient hostilities, some commentators argue that the opposite is more the case in the sense that what we think of as tribalism in Africa is a relatively modern development that emerged specifically as a result of external interventions. The spread and strengthening of kinship ties, which today we consider as 'tribalism' emerged to become a dominant way of political life as a consequence of the major slaving period in Africa (Ekeh,

1990). The long and painful trade in slaves from the ninth century when Arabs hunted for Africans to enslave through to the end of the European engagement in the trade in the nineteenth century, tribalism became a form of self-defence when the existing states failed to defend their citizens or collaborated with the slavers. As slave-trading African states became progressively predatory due to their dependence on the trade for their viability as exporters of captives for enslavement or importers of arms to pursue the trade, kinship systems were strengthened as a means of providing some form of protection against the brutality of the trade.

The ruin of Africans has some of its major roots in the Arab slave trade that spanned many centuries before the advent of the Europeans. The Arabs used terms such as 'abd' (Meyers (1977); Hamel (2014)) in relation to a black slave. The ancient but persistent view of Africans as slaves or inferior people in the Arab world has been at the core of some of the enduring violence between communities in Africa today as exemplified by the harrowing consequences of the near permanent conflict in the Sudan and elsewhere on the continent.

Postcolonial Entrenchment

The triumph of the Europeans over the Arabs in Africa and their subsequent domination of the continent brought to prominence the general use of the term 'tribe' at the dawn of the colonial age. The uses of the term were developed during the nineteenth century rise of racist evolutionary theories that permeated sociological and anthropological literature, which came to underpin the mind-set of the colonial project. It became a convenient administrative tool throughout the colonial era for the gathering of Africans into identifiable "tribes" by organising groups on the basis of linguistic and cultural similarities that were previously unimportant in order to simplify the problem of how to dominate and exploit the vast number of indigenous inhabitants. In other words, tribalism solved the colonial problem as it provided the means to 'divide and rule[35]' the inhabitants. The malevolent power of the tribal idea ultimately came to inform the post-colonial policies of the white South African government during the apartheid years.

Regrettably, the demise of colonial rule has done little to weaken 'tribal' consciousness, instead it continues to exert huge influences in the daily lives of Africans, fuelling individual and group competition within the artificial borders left behind by the colonial powers. Some political actors in post-colonial Africa have come to rely on the politics of 'divide and rule' to survive, which in many cases end in repressions, political killings and ultimately rebellions. The merciless rules of Mobutu in Zaire and Bokassa in Central African Republic among many others provide vivid examples. Decades after the demise of colonialism, Africans continue to face difficult challenges in maintaining peace and steady community development crucial for their existence and growth as their leaders often exploit so-called 'tribal' loyalties to advance their personal gains, narrow-minded interests, patronage and cronyism to the detriment of their communities at large. Consequently, the challenge for democracy among other key issues in Africa lies in the

---

[35] The idea of divide-and-rule describes a strategy for political actors or rulers to sustain power by fragmenting rival concentrations of power in ways that neutralizes powerful rivals.

use of identity politics to promote narrow 'tribal' interests.

Somalia provides a sharp heart-wrenching example of the dangers of building nations around clan identities instead of ideas. Since the end of the cold war much attention has been focused on removing autocratic African leaders and promoting multi-party politics, yet many African states have simply returned to maintaining 'tribal' identities as the basis for political attractiveness in the absence of commitments to build genuine political parties that compete on the basis of ideas. In essence, 'tribal' sensibilities inhibit the establishment of strong democratic institutions with tragic consequences as tribalistic interests continue to play a vicious role in armed conflict and civil disorder in numerous parts of the continent.

But how is it possible that African states having gained their freedom from colonial domination then consolidate their achievements in unhelpful ways along 'tribal' cleavages? One consideration could be drawn from the impact of the mode of decolonization in shaping postcolonial political institutions in Africa that left enduring imprints on the African approach to politics. For example, the transfer of power in many cases gave little room or support for democratic institutions promoting representation, consultation, involvement and participation of the people to become well established, and as a result unfortunately leading to the rise of numerous autocratic rulers across the continent. Arguably the conditions for such tyrannical modes of governing could be understood through the authoritarian and coercive rule of the colonial systems that the people experienced. It is helpful that we understand these colonial systems as involving not only the recent European domination in Africa but also the Arab control of Africans through Islam since ancient times to the present.

Let us revisit the Sudan, mentioned earlier in our discussion. The domination of the Sudan by the Arabized Islamic Sudanese has contributed to the production of tragic results far beyond comprehension and the ongoing war in the region can be included among the longest running conflicts in the world (Berkeley, 2001). The harrowing incidences of torture, rape, hunger, displacement and other senseless atrocities have come to acquire some sort of ease about it that the world is increasingly becoming indifferent to the engendered horrors. This numbing tragedy is truly overwhelming for African community leaders at large but it is their duty to play the leading role in bringing peace to alleviate the needless suffering of countless Africans.

Another potential crisis point for the future is how those states living along the Nile proceed with sharing its resources. The Nile is a lifeline for almost 400 million people, it is arguably the longest river in the world flowing through numerous African states before completing its approximately 7000 km journey from the highlands in the interior of the continent to the Mediterranean Ocean. The enduring tensions between the states along the Nile have some of their roots embedded in decisions made during the colonial period such as the 1929 agreement over the Nile between the British colonial power at the time and Egypt. An arrangement that continues to be a source of bitter disputes today long after the cessation of British colonial rule in Africa. The emergence of independent African states and hence new political realities together with the mounting economic and development pressures on these states are rapidly increasing the dispute over who owns the Nile. Egypt's resistance to reviewing the colonial agreement which favoured it to veto any development along the entire Nile water system that it deems a threat to its own water supply remains a huge hurdle for peaceful coexistence of all the states along the banks of this life giving river. Granted that there is a very serious possibility that without the Nile Egypt may cease to exist, as it happens to be the sole source of water supply for the Egyptians. However, it is contentious for Egypt to want to preserve and continue to enforce an agreement reached with a colonial power that once ruled over Egypt (and other areas of the African continent) but was in due course rejected by the Egyptians. It is not clear how long Egypt can continue to put so much faith in a colonial agreement that disregarded the needs of Africans living along the Nile who have today risen to assert their sovereign right to use their water resources for their own national development? Anwar Sadat's declaration in 1976 continues to clearly represent the Egyptian position that Egyptians depend totally on the Nile for survival and therefore they will not hesitate to go to war over access to the Nile (Okoth-Owiro, 2004). But how does this Egyptian position that is fixated on the survival of Egypt to the exclusion of the wellbeing of other Africans foster understanding and peaceful coexistence in sharing such a vital resources for all those living by the Nile? How does Egypt justify the diversion of the Nile to the Sinai region and building dams that have not only led to the loss of invaluable ancient artefacts but to the displacement of generations of Nubians with no clear policy of sharing the purported benefits of these projects with them? How justified is Egypt in its wishes to stop those African communities living along the Nile from exploiting the same resources? The River Nile problem presents a very strong case why real progress can only be made in Africa through a united and cooperative stance.

A Portrait of Unity

The issues considered beforehand outline some of the problems facing Africans today in terms of working together toward lasting peace and prosperity for all Africans. What would unity for Africans look like? The diversity that describes Africa offers a powerful creative force in shaping a positive future for Africans if they are ready to take on the challenge in harnessing the opportunities presented.

A number of studies (McLeod, Lobel and Cox, 1996; Bassett-Jones, 2005; Phillips[36], 2014) have suggested the importance of diversity as a potential source of creative and competitive advantage. They revealed how

---

[36] Philips maintains that when people are brought together in a group to solve problems they bring different information, opinions and perspectives unique to bear on the task at hand with the potential of producing the very best results, and diversity in such instances help to move participants into cognitive action in ways that homogeneity simply does not. According to Phillips, members of a homogeneous group are somewhat assured that they will agree with one another, in other words, that they will understand one another's perspectives and beliefs and assume that they will be able to easily come to a consensus. However, when members of a group notice that they are socially different from one another, they change their expectations as they anticipate differences of opinion and perspective. They assume they will need to work harder to come to a consensus. This logic, argues Phillips, helps to explain both the positive and the negative aspects of social diversity that people work harder in diverse environments both cognitively and socially, and in spite of the possibilities that they might not like it, the difficulties they work through nevertheless can lead to better outcomes.

heterogeneity of ethnicity enhanced group creativity and its potential performance advantages over homogeneous groups if the conflict-increasing influence of heterogeneity were combined with good working relationships.

What is indicative is the importance of diversity in enhancing the creative process. However, due to its power to damage cohesiveness a key factor to gaining maximum group performance is the proper management of diversity. The suitable management style needed therefore can only be explained through the quality of leadership that is brought to bear on the handling of diversity within a group or community.

Diversity in relation to Africa can be viewed as presenting great opportunities for innovation and development if the right conditions are encouraged. Let us consider such a situation in the case of the Nile discussed earlier. As already indicated, currently the various African states situated along the Nile are pursuing different goals regarding their utilisation of the river and thus making it difficult for any meaningful and durable consensus. The Egyptians being one of the key players in the discussions present a significant case to be addressed by all the states sharing the river. Considering the absolute dependence of Egypt on the River Nile for its existence it is very difficult to envisage how Egypt could continue to survive without some kind of special provision. The issue of how best the resources of the Nile can be shared highlights one of the key challenges for Africans. The differences among the people of Africa that have been accentuated over the centuries by local as well as foreign forces continue to negatively impact in a number of ways in the seeking of solutions to dire issues affecting Africans.

As already indicated, Egypt draws its supposed legitimacy for controlling the Nile from a colonial agreement which bears no meaningful advantages for the states along the Nile that have since come into existence including South Sudan the newest African state. At the time of the 1929 Nile agreement Britain was the undisputed colonial power controlling most of the entire length of the river from the heart of Africa to the Mediterranean Sea and as such, decisions on issues at the time were often made and actions unwaveringly taken without the consultation or consent of those communities most affected by such decisions. The long-term ramifications of the policy in terms of its potential to exacerbate tensions between neighbouring Nile communities is dangerously real. In spite of its perilous situation concerning access to water, Egypt's approach to the issues of sharing the Nile water betrays a lack of sensitivity to the needs of those communities living closer to the source of the Nile, and by doing so appear to demonstrate what might seem to be contempt for these communities. But how long will it take the Egyptians to come to the realisation that the 1929 British agreement in its original format is no longer binding in the present time with regard to the new sovereign states upstream who now desire to exploit the resources of the river for their own betterment? Is waging war, as indicated by Anwar Sadat the answer to any long-term durable solution to a problem that in the future is surely bound to get more complicated due to population growth and the need for development upstream along the Nile?

The Nile problem as already mentioned presents one clear opportunity for the communities sharing the river to collaborate closely in their search for common solutions. It has the potential to inspire the communities to work toward economic and political harmony as a means to sharing their common resources and diverse cultures. Egypt in particular, stands to gain as its only means of survival is based on the adequate flow of the Nile. But how can this be done? The communities can begin by considering how the existing dams along the river can be shared without the need for more dams to be built, as the future consequences for the proliferation of dams are incalculable. While the benefits of dams in promoting industrial development have always provided the raison d'être for their undertaking, the long-term effects of such industrial endeavours as already considered in our earlier discussions remain to be given widespread exposure to emphasise their negative effects on rivers and on surrounding communities whose livelihoods depend on it.

The importance of good, committed and efficient leadership in managing such diversity that underscores the African milieu cannot be over stated. How decent and how glorious it could be for the African states along the Nile to pull together in sharing the vast resources of the river. A successful alliance when established could be extended across the African continent. Despite the benefits of such collaborations they remain very challenging to attain. In view of the elusiveness of clear productive cooperation among Africans how are we to consider the African future?

PART THREE

IMAGINING THE AFRICAN FUTURE

The catchphrase 'Africa Rising' became a very fashionable promotional device in the past few years to highlight and promote a turning point in the perceived development for a brighter future in Africa. But while the success stories have focused on, and elevated some African states and individuals, many more continue to suffer and in the light of the on-going African condition how shall we begin to imagine the future for Africa?

CHAPTER SEVEN

AT THE CROSSROADS

Like rock stratification, African issues are layered and extend far back into antiquity. If Africa is to be successful then it must struggle to overcome the inherent inflexibilities that have constrained necessary positive progress. But how can this be done in the midst of the enduring distractions, tensions and conflicts? In some sense Africa has completed a full circle to arrive at the crossroads today at the beginning of the twenty-first century and must face the arduous task of making choices that will undoubtedly shape its progress into the foreseeable future or succumb to a fresh cycle of enslavement and ultimate destruction.

Choices

The rule of brutal despots and oppressive illegitimate regimes in the cold war era somehow morphed into democratic regimes as a consequence of the post-cold war political changes forced by the rise of democracy across the world. However, the change to multi-party political systems in Africa does not appear to have made any great difference in the desires of many African leaders. Once they gain political power they attempt to manipulate the system in order to entrench their rule by remaining in office beyond the limits of their official terms. It appears the change is yet to be successful in curbing the tenacity of cronyism, partiality, corruption and patrimonial politics, which continue to undermine vital state institutions and the rule of law essential for the efficient operation of any democratic system of government. Considering their weaknesses, the ramifications for these vital institutions mean that decisions concerning development projects fail to undergo the thorough examination needed before they are implemented as well as the required robust monitoring after their implementation. A concise example can be drawn from Ghana involving the upgrading of one of the important road networks in the capital, Accra that cost the nation 18 million dollars.

Giffard Road covers a distance of approximately 6km and until 2013 was a single lane tree-lined road. Sections of the road have always been very active as transport hubs, business centres, beer bars, day and night food stalls and general provisions markets. All theses enterprises served the communities living on both sides of the road. The significance of Giffard Road is in its use as part of a network of ceremonial roads in Accra along which presidents and dignitaries visiting the capital are often driven. The reconstruction of the road involved the Chinese and the work that ensued was aimed at expanding the road from a single lane to multiple lanes. Consequently, the first to be destroyed before the commencement of the work were all the trees along the existing road. The work, which was planned for completion in eighteen months, took twice the time, and remains to be fully completed as points for pedestrian crossings and all the street lighting are yet to be fully functioning. The shoddiness in the planning became evident in the construction process and in the quality of the completed road.

While the road has now been widened, it has introduced some new difficulties for both motorists and pedestrians. For example, due to lack of parking facilities motorists are forced to use pedestrian designated pathways, moreover safe pedestrian crossings hardly exist for able and disable pedestrians resulting in the increase in fatal and near fatal accidents. Ironically, Giffard Road, which was once a relatively safe and easy road for pedestrians and motorists to use has now become hostile to the community that it is meant to serve.

If the improvement work done on Giffard Road can serve as an indication of how development work is carried out in Ghana then the situation presents an alarming course for concern. Considering the millions of dollars borrowed from foreign banks on behalf of the citizens for the work, it is very reasonable to expect that any work carried out is never done at a sub-standard level by ensuring quality supervision and monitoring at all stages for desirable outcomes. How can Ghana or Africa in general truly progress by not rising above the mediocre or sub-standard level of doing things? When are Africans going to regain the confidence to take total charge of their own development projects from conception through financing to their glorious delivery? How will Africans come to produce their own essential things if they offer themselves no incentives nor create the opportunities to engage in such production enterprises?

For so long Africa has existed mainly as a consumer oriented world with very marginal contribution to the production of goods and services for export and local consumption, but is this a tenable choice for Africa to maintain for now and into the foreseeable future? Much of Africa's engagement in production is in terms of extraction of its abundant natural resources but is this sufficient to assure a reasonable level of prosperity indefinitely? On the contrary, when one observes Africa with its abundant resources it is striking how poverty is persistently rife among the people. But why is this so? Many of the problems can be located in the choices that Africans, particularly their leaders, make on behalf of their people. Admittedly, African leaders contributed to the betrayal of the visions of self-determination, prosperity and peace that underscored the African post-colonial renewal, which continues to influence decisions and events on the continent. For decades in post-colonial Africa power remained in the hands of those with guns and not those with the vision, intelligence and determination for nation building, a condition that continues to impact on Africa's development. While African leaders give much lip service to the importance of education, inadequate actions are taken to commit substantial national resources to the acquisition and enhancement of knowledge and skills for development, for example in science and technology. Yet the transformative power of intellectual capital in wealth creation is unequivocal. It is arguable in the African context that investments in intellectual development in the long term, for example, outweigh the focus on the extraction of natural resources simply as raw materials for export. In other words, Africa's future survival lies in the development of the capacity for producing goods and services to compete on the world market. What is clearly unsustainable for Africa is that it cannot continue to exist merely as a consumer society if its people are to be lifted out of their current poverty trap. As Chinese goods and services for example, pour into Africa at a relentless pace and in competition with other world producers, Africa is indeed at the crossroads in terms of how it positions itself in the world as choices must be made willingly or reluctantly. Bennett (1993) deftly expressed the situation:

> A nation is a *choice*. It chooses itself at fateful forks in the road by turning left or right, by giving something or taking something – and in the giving up and the taking, in the deciding and not deciding, the nation *becomes*. And ever afterwards, the nation and the people who make up the nation are defined by the fork and by the decision that was made there, as well as by the decision that was not made there (p61).

Africans can no longer pass on the responsibility for their continuing predicament beyond the actions and performances of their leaders and therefore must hold them strictly accountable for the choices they make on their behalf. Africans must rise up and remain vigilant, as the future for Africa if it remains on its current trajectory may perhaps have nothing left to offer them but the choice of how to die.

Facing Extinction?

The seriousness of severe poverty and degradation in Africa cannot be exaggerated. While the notion of extinction may be viewed as too pessimistic, the embellished idea of 'Africa Rising' is not helpful. For a large section of the African population the reality of everyday living is presented in the struggle to obtain one decent meal each day. It is absurd that for a people so potentially powerful, whose land is potentially the richest on earth, number greatly among the poorest people on the face of the earth.

Who is managing the African wealth? The question concerning the recalcitrant problem of poverty in Africa is open to endless debate while the suffering continues unabated, and is likely to escalate considering our earlier discussions.   Issues concerning ownership of resources remain a serious threat to the survival of the continent and its people.   For example, over the past decade or so, interest in the acquisition of land escalated in numerous parts of Africa resulting in pressures on small local farmers and landowners who often play a critical role in feeding African communities across the continent.   What has become the trend is that African leaders   facilitate   joint   ventures   between   their governments and giant foreign companies that ironically result in the displacement of local farmers[37] in spite of the often-intended broad objectives to create jobs and growth. Large land deals between African governments and foreign investors seriously threaten the existence of local farmers, as portions of the African countryside are leased or concessioned often for as long as 50 to 99years. Lands considered available have changed owners with frightening implications for the local people   and   their   environment.   With   estimates approaching   227   million   hectares   globally   and approximately 70% of the total in Africa[38], what is inevitably taking place is the transformation of landholdings that has given rise to strong opposing

[37] The Guardian report http://www.theguardian.com/global-development-professionals-network/2015/mar/13/african-land-grabs-companies--financiers-regulation

[38] The Guardian report http://www.theguardian.com/global-development-professionals-network/2014/jan/23/land-deals-africa-farming-investment

factions, one stressing the advantages and the other the disadvantages.

Although evidence for the implications of land deals for the African people presents a very complex situation (Cotula, 2013) with no credible direction of future ramifications as important data necessary for establishing clear trends are not easily obtainable. However, the existing evidence as already mentioned indicates that the traditional small scale African farmer is in deadly danger of being crushed under the mighty boots of giant international agribusiness firms as they march across Africa in search of well-endowed lands to expand their business dealings and ultimately their profit margins. Amanor (2012), an eminent African scholar on land issues in Africa, outlined the situation in his observation that the small African agricultural producers are unable to compete and are consequently pushed out of production due to the severe global market forces in operation. It may not be entirely absurd to imagine the passing of the small-scale farmer in Africa who has traditionally been critical in the production of food if African governments provide no reasonable support for their continuing survival in the presence of the powerful global market pressures under which they are forced to operate.

After centuries of foreign companies harnessing African resources and in some instances in association with local African partners, the challenge remains for obtaining evidence to support the positive benefits that accrued for the average African from antiquity to our present time. The desirability of African lands has its beginnings in antiquity, and as history tells us, it is arguable that the successive foreign penetrations in Africa since then merely contributed to the considerable problems existing in Africa. Indeed, from a Diopian[39] perspective Africa is often the giver in the encounter with foreign forces. Presently, Africa continues to give of its natural resources in ways that could be viewed as having little positive impact on most Africans; yet it is, paradoxically, being touted as the future breadbasket[40] of the world. But how long can it continue to do so into the foreseeable future without harming the African people? The vulnerability of majority of Africans facing an uncertain future with regard to growing population, poverty and its crippling consequences, land degradation, predicted climatic effects and a whole host of issues that continue to present challenges is emphatically intense.

Why the on-going suffering of the African people amid the abundance of resources? One cannot help turning repeatedly to such a question and labouring the issue in spite of our previous discussions. A large population of the African youth of today are conscious of the bleakness of their conditions and are consequently prepared to escape it by any means possible. The confusion in Africa that has led to unceasing conflicts in some parts, economic failure in others and the exclusions of communities yet in some quarters have left the youth seeking refuge and better opportunities elsewhere. The trickle of Africans across the Sahara desert heading north with the hope of reaching Europe has turned into a tragedy as Africans die en route or drown in the Mediterranean Sea in their frantic attempts to enter Europe. Furthermore, a very disturbing issue is the resounding silence that African leaders have chosen to

---

[39] In his writings on the African origin of civilization, Cheikh Anta Diop suggests that no foreign invaders in antiquity brought civilization to pharaonic Egypt
[40] National Geographic report
http://www.nationalgeographic.com/foodfeatures/land-grab/

maintain in the midst of the raging catastrophe. Why have the leaders of Africa abandoned their own sons and daughters to their doom in foreign lands? Whose responsibility is it to safeguard the wellbeing of the next generation of Africans today?

The Leadership Tragedy

Failure of leadership in Africa is at the core of the hopelessness among the youth of Africa today and a critical factor in what becomes of the African world in the distant future. Recognition of the widespread and real crises of leadership motivated the creation of The African Leadership Forum in 1988 under the auspices of the Nigerian president at the time Olusegun Obasanjo to address the development of leadership in Africa in order to increase the effectiveness of major actors in government and civil society across the continent. In the Forum's inaugural programme[41] key discussions on economic and social issues together with those of political and strategic concerns where highlighted. It was noted that a very important factor that contributed to the numerous setbacks and failures of leadership since independence is the perpetuation of inherited colonial structures, which are often ineffective. Furthermore, the continuing fragmentation, instability and external control of the development process, and poor infrastructures resulting in the exploitation and concentration of the benefits from development in the hands of a few African leaders. The problems of corruption at all levels and the general cynicism towards government affairs were noted as critical issues. It also

---

[41] See The Challenges of Leadership in African Development
http://www.africaleadership.org/rc/the%20challenges%20of%20leadership %20in%20africa%20development.pdf

highlighted the attitude of contempt and disregard that African leaders tend to display even as they claim to govern in the name of the people. These were some of the dire issues of leadership that gave impetus to the establishment of the Forum as an expression of commitment to contributing in a constructive and positive way to the search for solutions to some of these leadership problems in order to create conditions for the development of the continent in an environment of peace, stability and security.

However, many decades after the supposed creation of the Forum the problem of abuse of the African people and disrespect for their human dignity by their contemptuous leaders remains a colossal setback. What has been the impact of the Forum, which was meant to be the 'Damascus Road' conversion in African development efforts? The fact that it has made negligible impact and sunk without trace tells us all we need to know about the seriousness of purpose with which African leaders approach our problems.

In his intimate dairy entries during his 1965 sojourn in Congo participating in revolutionary activates to assist the Congolese to throw off the yoke of imperialism, Ernesto 'Che' Guevara (2001) provides some revealing aspects of African leadership. Throughout the difficult months that year he spent in the dense African jungle sleeping on bare, hard and rough ground, eating the simple meals of the local people, contracting fever and dysentery, engaging with imperialist forces in skirmishes and providing medical attention to the wounded, Guevara noted a number of traits that characterized the leadership to which he was offering his assistance. His first observation pointed to the self-centeredness and lack of unity among the leaders. At a meeting that he addressed during his first official visit to Tanzania, Guevara had great difficulties trying to explain to the leaders of the various liberation movements who gathered to request for financial assistance and personal training in Cuba that a revolutionary solder cannot be trained in an academy but can only be formed in warfare. He tried to reason with them considering the struggle was in Africa:

> I therefore suggested that training should take place not in our far away Cuba but in the nearby Congo, where the struggle was not against some puppet like Tshombe but against North American imperialism, which, in its neo-colonial form, was threatening the newly acquired independence of nearly every African people or helping to keep the colonies in subjugation. I spoke to them of the fundamental importance which the Congo liberation struggle had in our eyes. Victory would be continental in its reach and its consequence, and so would defeat.
>
> The reaction was worse than cool. Although most refrained from any kind of comment, some asked to speak and took me violently to task for the advice I had given. They argued that their respective peoples, who had been abused and degraded by imperialism, would protest if any casualties were suffered not as a result of oppression in their own land, but from a war to liberate another country. I tried to show them that we were talking not of a struggle within fixed frontiers, but of a war against the common enemy, present as much in Mozambique as in Malawi, Rhodesia or South Africa, the Congo or Angola. No one saw it like that (p7).

It is telling to note how the opposition Guevara experienced in attempting to persuade the Africans to pull their resources together as a unified force to combat the forces of imperialism illuminates the resistance Nkrumah faced as his explanations and appeals for Africans to come together fell on deaf ears. The now legendary self-serving and corrupt attitude of many

African leaders is a significant ingredient in the African development failures.

In spite of his encounter with these African leaders, Guevara nonetheless persevered with his plan to assist in the struggle by going on to the battlefront in the Congolese jungle and there the failure of leadership again was expressed in the chronic disorganization:

> Right from the start, we came face to face with a reality that would pursue us through the struggle: the lack of organization (p11).

The inability to plan ahead for possible eventualities and the concomitant disorder that can ensue underpin incompetent leadership. Guevara witnessed firsthand how such incompetent leadership was masked by the Congolese fighters belief in sorcery rather than meticulous planning:

> This *dawa,* which did quite a lot of damage to military preparations, operates according to the following principle. A liquid in which herb juices and other magical substances have been dissolved is thrown over the fighter, and certain occult signs – nearly always including a coal mark on the forehead – are administered to him. This protects him against all kinds of weapons (although the enemy too relies upon magic), but he must not lay hands on anything that does not belong to him, or touch a woman, or feel fear, on pain of losing the protection. The answer to any transgression is very simple: a man dead = a man who took fright, stole or slept with a woman; a man wounded = a man who was afraid. Since fear accompanies wartime operations, fighters found it quite natural to attribute wounds to faintheartedness – that is, to lack of belief. And the dead do not speak; all three faults can be ascribed to them.
>
> The belief is so strong that no one goes into battle without having the *dawa* performed. I was constantly afraid that this superstition would rebound against us, that we would

> be blamed for any military disaster involving many deaths. I
> tried several times to have a talk about the *dawa* with some
> in a position of responsibility, so that an effort could be
> started to win people away from it – but it was impossible.
> The *dawa* is treated as an article of faith. The most
> politically advanced say that it is a natural, material force,
> and that they, as dialectical materialists recognize its power
> and the secrets held by the medicine men in the jungle (p14
> -15).

On one occasion, Guevara asked the medicine man to go to the battlefront with the fighters but the medicine man cleverly refused by saying stronger magic portions can be prepared for the fighters. While it is acceptable to seek to bolster the morale of fighters for battle by any means, none can replace the training and detailed planning that must go into the preparations for any battle, a responsibility that forms a crucial aspect of good leadership.

Throughout his stay in the jungle the high command of the liberation fighters paid scant visits to the action zones to train, organize and lead the fighters from the front as they spent much of the time elsewhere allegedly in meetings or on international travels. This lack of attention from the leaders also helped to exacerbate the indiscipline, laziness and demoralizing stance of the fighters. The corrupt attitude of the leaders left Guevara in no doubt that Africa had a long way to go to reach real revolutionary maturity. Guevara's account provides a helpful illustration of some of the leadership failures that Africans must muster the courage to address.

The future for Africa remains a perilous challenge considering the leadership issues that it continues to face in a world that has grown exceedingly complex over the last five decades. Consequently, Africa's survival or extinction will in some way depend on the kind of future leaders that emerge.

What kind of leadership is needed to positively mitigate the potentially catastrophic problems that Africa faces? A new generation of leaders (Igue, 2010) who are capable of facing up to such challenges as the fragmentation of the continent, the promotion of democracy and human rights and the implementation of new conditions for peace and freedom among others must be considered. In addition, an essential element in the character of such new leadership must also include a total commitment to a Pan-African sensitivity and approach informed by a higher ethical understanding of the African predicament and the depth of responsibility that is demanded.

CHAPTER EIGHT

RESPONSIBILITY

Regardless of how we view the African situation, the onus firmly rests on Africans to lead the search for successful and enduring solutions to the myriad and complex problems that continue to challenge Africa. In other words, it is only through the firm and unconditional commitment of African leaders to care for the African people that real positive change can be firmly established on the continent.

Predecessors

Africa's devastated past and the associated difficulties in its recovery need no further sustained elaboration. However, in view of the importance of helpful historical references to fortify future leadership, how might we begin to ascertain some of the required essential factors for encouraging a new breed of dedicated and caring African leaders to lift the continent and its people out of the persistent wretchedness that has come to define what it means to be African in our present time? How are Africans to approach the monumental task of reengaging with their past in order to help them chart a more productive future?

We can begin by viewing Africa from three perspectives. We can take the first period as dating as far back from antiquity through to the end of the Pharaonic era. The second period spans the very long and difficult period of the destruction and domination of Africa by Asian and European forces. The third epoch is defined by the period of decolonization of Africa from foreign domination to our present time of independent Africa.

Considering the significance of Africa's pre-colonial era, the notion generally held by some non-African commentators that it gave little of significance to world history has been one of the main pillars that some of the most illustrious intellectuals of African descent through the times have fought to reject. Indeed today the persistence of the dearth of important and uncontroversial knowledge of Africa's contribution to the civilisation of humankind remains the case in many centres of education in the African world. A situation that greatly impacts not all together positively on the knowledge and confidence that some of African descent today have of who they are and how they relate to, and draw inspiration from their past. One cannot begin without some sense of appreciation and acknowledgement of the civilizations that emerged along the River Nile as forming the pinnacle of the various civilizations that were produced by Africans. During this period the Nile valley civilization in Egypt ascended to the highest stage in Africa. It is from this point in antiquity that future African leaders must begin the reconstruction of their understanding of the colossal tasks that they face in the decolonization and development of the continent.

The conquest and expropriation of African civilization that underscored the long and difficult period of its destruction by Asian and European forces if properly understood, can provide a solid foundation on which future African leaders can learn to broaden their understanding of the nature and scope of the subjugation under which Africans existed. It is this period in the history of Africa that continues to shape the perceptions and the received realities of Africans. A deep appreciation of the impact of this period on Africa's progression path is critical for the informed future African leader.

Although Africa is viewed today as independent and free from any form of domination it nevertheless continues to experience some conditions reminiscent of those in the period of its destruction and colonization. After half a century or so of uninterrupted independence in Africa, we are in a privileged position with hindsight to examine, as already suggested in our discussions, progress so far made and the lessons that this might have for future Africa leaders.

The leaders that spearheaded the demand for the liberation of Africans from foreign domination generally had their objectives somewhat well defined by the nature of the struggle and the enemies that they opposed. In other words, their struggle was against the colonial system and its treatment of Africans in their own homelands as second-rate citizens, and their enemies were the individuals and groups that profited from the system. These leaders made great sacrifices often involving the foregoing of their own personal enjoyment as provided in the home comfort of a wife and children for the cause of liberating their people. Some lost their youth and best years to lengthy jail sentences as it was in the case of Nelson Mandela[42], and others like Amilcar Cabral[43], Patrice Lumumba[44] and Toussaint L'Ouverture[45] made the ultimate sacrifice in giving their lives for the struggle.

The sacrifices made by the liberation leaders were genuine and resolute, and the struggle was generally understood and supported by the African masses, which ultimately led to the granting of independence across Africa. However, the clarity of the objective, which underpinned and defined the success of the liberation movements in Africa, was no longer the case in the warm refreshing glow of the trappings of freedom on the one hand, and the implicit responsibility demanded by independence on the other hand. The covert disagreements and lack of cooperation that emerged among some leaders of the newly liberated areas of the African world did much to destroy the progress that could have been made particularly in terms of cooperation and unity in fighting a common purpose for development and the establishment of human dignity for all Africans. Moreover, the mentality of non-cooperation and disunity defeated the pleas for unity and cooperation. Since then the ensuing outcome has been the slow but persisting descent of the African world into corruption and abuse of power by some of its leaders through unending conflicts, violence and brutalities, lack of genuine development of infrastructure and above all the abandonment of the uplift of the African people. The resulting loss of development opportunities as a consequence of the

---

[42] The undisputed leader of the struggle against the system of Apartheid in South Africa.

[43] Revolutionary leader for the independence of Guinea-Bissau and Cape Verde Island.

[44] Congolese independence leader.

[45] Haitian independence revolutionary leader.

failings of the African liberation leaders motivated by their politics of betrayal has found fertile ground to drive down deeper roots in the machinations of the current generation of African leaders. The wretchedness of the situation as perceptively observed by Bayart (2014) is how the consciousness of wanton inequality has normalised corruption for the African people as a method of social resistance to the daily oppressive economic conditions that they suffer. In other words, the poor majority adopt the dishonest practices employed by their leaders to steal and accumulate wealth and power as a technique for their own survival.

Africa now faces a new and treacherous tyranny spearheaded by dreadful and dishonest African leaders. This situation calls for a renewed revolutionary struggle by the African people to demand from their leaders the responsibility for delivering their dignity and human rights entitlements expressed in the visions of social and economic opportunities that can be made available to all.

Manifesting the Visions

Total self-reliance is unquestionably the price of freedom, and the point that Africans must learn to rely on themselves has been passionately presented and defended in the writings of Nkrumah and Diop.

Puzzling Poverty

Having already argued powerfully for continental African unity, Nkrumah (2004) attempted to explain and caution Africans about the insidious and complex workings of international monopoly capital in Africa in his book *Neo-Colonialism.* First published over fifty years ago, it still remains relevant in some important aspects in the twenty-first century. Neo-colonialism, a political term used by Nkrumah to analyse the nature and workings of the exploitative system of economic and political control employed by the capitalist Western nations to dominate the developing world. In his introduction, he explains:

> The essence of neo-colonialism is that the state which is subject to it is, in theory, independent and has all the outward trappings of international sovereignty. In reality its economic system and thus its political policy is directed from outside.
>
> The method and form of this direction can take various shapes. For example, in an extreme case the troops of the imperial power may garrison the territory of the neo-colonial State and control the government of it. More often, however, neo-colonialist control is exercised through economic or monetary means (p.ix).

For Nkrumah the State is often the power exercising control where neo-colonialism exists, however, he points out:

> It is possible that neo-colonial control may be exercised by a consortium of financial interests which are not identifiable with any particular state (p.x).

This description truly resonates with our present understanding from the neo-liberal[46] perspective of the indomitable power of transnational corporations not only in Africa but also across the developing world. It is ironic that a few years before Nkrumah wrote his book, John Kennedy, the American president warned Americans in 1961 about the dangers they face from a monolithic and ruthless conspiracy that relies primarily on covert means to expand its realm of influence:

> It is a system which has conscripted vast human and material resources into the building of a tightly knit, highly efficient machine that combines military, diplomatic, intelligence, economic, scientific and political operations[47].

The irony is that while Nkrumah was trying to address the issues of Africa's underdevelopment due to imperialist forces, which extended to American operations, Kennedy was underlining the dangers posed by a covert scheme against the American people. Could it be that both leaders were faced with the same forces but in different circumstances?

For Nkrumah neo-colonialism resulted in the use of foreign capital for the exploitation rather than the development of the less developed areas of the world, and as a consequence, it deepens the gap between the rich and poor countries. Although Nkrumah viewed the neo-colonial system from a perspective mainly focused on Africa, however, the similarities today with the neo-liberal ideology which has now resulted in some

---

[46] Neoliberalism is the ideology and policy model that involves the systemic transfer of economic factors and power from the public sector to the private sector.

[47] See speech given to publishers at
http://www.jfklibrary.org/Research/Research-Aids/JFK-Speeches/American-Newspaper-Publishers-Association_19610427.aspx

Western countries such as Greece[48] undergoing comparable exploitative outcomes as in the developing world demonstrates the depth of the problem the world faces. Nkrumah was far-sighted in his characterisation of the system as:

> For those who practise it, it means power without responsibility and for those who suffer from it, it means exploitation without redress (p.xi).

Since Nkrumah's time the state of exploitation without redress has not fundamentally changed but now parade itself in the guise of free market forces. He naturally viewed neo-colonialism as a major external force with the vested interest in keeping Africa underdeveloped but current conditions in Africa however, suggest a far more complex situation as some sections of the African leadership through corruption, mismanagement and tyranny add to the continuing exploitation and extreme poverty that remains the unacceptable plight of the African people. Nkrumah's belief that Africa can only be developed through a struggle against the external forces is correct but in view of present conditions in Africa it now needs to be extended to include a struggle against internal African forces that contribute to the continuing degradation of Africa.

The puzzling poverty in Africa despite the continent's immense resources continues to raise questions long after Nkrumah highlighted the workings of groups and individuals who operate to deepen Africa's impoverishment. Without over emphasising the point that Africa could be among the most advanced

---

[48] See the Greek Debt Truth Commission on Public Debt:
<http://greekdebttruthcommission.org/assets/porisma2_en.pdf

continents if its resources were harnessed and used for African development, its people still remain among some of the poorest in the twenty-first century. The obstacles to economic development in Africa according to Nkrumah are mainly due to the Balkanisation of the African continent. For Nkrumah, the disunity of African states is at the root of the uneven development on the continent. In other words, the continuing domination of Africa's economy by foreign firms must be ended if Africa is to achieve economic growth and this can only be done through a unified action. Nkrumah's persistent plea for African cooperation is informed by the trends in the world toward larger economic and political units as interdependence of nations grow:

> No country can be completely self-sufficient or afford to ignore political events outside of its borders. Africa is clearly fragmented into too many small, uneconomic and nonviable states, many of whom are having a very hard struggle to survive (p25).

If we observe these small African states today that based their development on narrow national considerations, many have made little progress half a century after decolonisation in Africa. The evidence sustains Nkrumah's argument for a unified and continentally planned economic survival and growth, secured by mutual benefits from industrialisation and the lifting of the mass of Africans from poverty made possible by a common purpose and direction:

> The richer countries would be able to help the poorer. Resources can be pooled and development projects co-ordinated to raise the living standard of every African (p26).

If Africa is to achieve rounded economic wellbeing it must end the domination of its economy by foreign investors, which now includes Chinese and other Asian financiers. For Nkrumah this could only be done in a new revolutionary way and could not emphasis the situation enough:

> Something in the nature of an economic revolution is required. Our development has been held back for too long by the colonial type economy. We need to reorganise entirely so that each country can specialise in producing the goods and crops for which it is best suited (p27).

Towards such a revolution every African state has some contribution to make to the economic whole from its resource location on the continent. However, for economic unity to be effective, Nkrumah warned that it must be accompanied by political unity, as the two are intertwined and essential for the future greatness of Africa. Sadly, what still remains a problem is the will to unite and cooperate towards the eradication of the extreme conditions of poverty in Africa.

Cooperation

The essential nature and factors underpinning the poverty and degradation of Africans in the midst of their vast resources, as argued by Nkrumah, can be found in the exploitative economic and political relationship between Africa and its foreign investors. In strengthening the case towards the advantages of African cooperation, Diop (1987) presented a convincing argument for the industrialisation of Africa by highlighting the cultural and economic basis for realising such a project.

Diop begins by placing the utmost importance on the historical unity of Africans highlighting the interconnectedness of their genealogy from prehistoric period to the present. For Diop, Africans today are in no way invaders from another continent and can therefore be considered the original inhabitants as scientific discoveries show Africa to be the cradle of humanity. Accordingly, the geographical and psychological unity that binds Africans is an elementary fact. Diop argues that the structure of the pre-colonial African family, that of the State and the associated philosophical and moral concepts reveals a consistent cultural unity as a result of similar adaptations to the same material and physical conditions of life. Furthermore, Diop maintains that there is a common linguistic background connecting African languages to one linguistic family. While an African union is conceivable on the basis of historical, geographical and economic unity, Diop contends that in order to complete such unity and set it on a modern autochthonous cultural base it will be necessary to recreate linguistic unity through the choice of an appropriate African language promoted to the influence of a modern cultural language. However, Diop believed:

> The choice of such language will have to be made by a competent interterritorial commission imbued with deep patriotic feeling foreswearing and hidden chauvinism (p11).

Africans have made negligible progress in the direction of adopting and promoting one African language as envisage by Diop. However, it must be acknowledged that the challenges in tackling this particular issue are by no means easy.

The significant perspective that Diop forcibly brings to the discussions of African cooperation is his explanation of the importance of the cultural unity of Africans. In contrast, but nonetheless supportive of Nkrumah's implicit assumptions of the cultural factors in his arguments for African unity, Diop attempts to provide meticulous account for the interconnectedness of the African people. On this basis Diop proceeded to formulate his vision for the industrial development of Africa by identifying the existence of eight natural zones based on the combined concentration of energy sources and raw materials across the continent.

The first zone constitutes the River Congo basin, which holds the potential to be the leading industrial region of Africa with its mighty reserves of hydraulic energy. By harnessing it to supply all the electricity needed for the various branches of industry it could be the principal centre for Africa's heavy industry. The gulf of Benin region comprising Nigeria, Benin and Cameroon make up the second zone with hydraulic reserves to power a major industrial hub for the continent. The third zone consists of Ghana and Ivory Coast, which together can use their forest reserves essentially for chemical utilization in addition to their sizable energy reserves. The fourth zone includes Guinea, Sierra Leone and Liberia. In addition to their energy reserves, this is a metallurgical region of the highest quality ideal for the installation of a powerful combine to serve the continent. The fifth is the tropical zone consisting of Senegal, Mali and Niger. The region was supposed to be energy-deficient at the time when Diop was outlining the future scope for a united Africa. However, the situation has changed significantly five decades later with the exploration and discovery of oil as predicted by Diop, but sadly not directed towards the establishment of thermal power plants and the availability of the necessary raw materials for a petrochemical industry as he envisaged. The Nilotic Sudan, the Great Lakes and Ethiopia, an area several times the size of Europe form the sixth zone. It is rich in hydraulic energy in addition to the potential deposits of uranium. It also has the potential to become a great naval construction region. With its asset of having the whole range of climatic zones it is well placed for diverse agricultural products and tourism. The seventh zone covers the Zambezi River basin with its vast energy reserves, uranium deposits and huge coal supplies. The eighth zone is South Africa, which has already been industrialised by the European minority inhabitants.

As envisaged by Diop, these zones with all their abundance of energy reserves and other natural resources capable of providing all the necessary advantages for Africa's industrialization have sadly not been efficiently exploited by Africans. Today, the lack of interstate cooperation in Africa as each state pursues its own development goals has resulted in the retardation of the continent's overall progress, with negative impact on the wellbeing of the vast majority of Africans that desperately need lifting out of poverty and degradation.

In highlighting some of the problems in achieving the success of economic and cultural cooperation in Africa Diop was clear about how his generation would be judged by future generations if they fail to bear the responsibility of bringing to fruition African unity and prosperity:

> Historical circumstances now demand of our generation that it solve in a felicitous manner the vital problems that face Africa, most especially the cultural problem. If we do not succeed in this, we will appear in the history of the development of our people as the watershed generation that was unable to ensure the unified cultural survival of the African continent; the generation which, out of political and intellectual blindness, committed the error fatal to our national future. We will have been the unworthy generation *par excellence* (p14).

Diop clearly understood the magnitude of the problems facing the continent and the degree of commitment and unselfishness needed to solve these difficult and deeply entrenched problems. Sadly, he does not have much faith in the dedication of those in power to tackle the issues:

> Those in political power are the only ones who have not proved themselves up to coping with these problems, who indeed have never seriously given thought to them, who are terrified of taking the action which they conceive as economic weaning. They rather attempt, while acting as a screen, to perpetuate the same old economic/political guardianship in a more insidious manner, less visible to the masses but no less effective (p16).

His lack of confidence in the commitment of African politicians to solve the chronic problems destroying the African people has been vindicated by the present economic and political state of the African continent. Without the show of responsibility expressed in unity to defeat common problems then the survival of the African people will continue to be open to grave and increasing levels of danger that only point to suffering and degradation in spite of the abundance of material resources.

CHAPTER NINE

SHAPING A POSITIVE FUTURE

What more can we say about the future for Africa considering the trajectory of its development over the past fifty years or so after centuries of colonial domination?

The evidence signposting Africa's development challenges cannot be over stated. It is clearly reinforced by the level of poverty across the continent, underlined by the lack of adequate medical care for most ordinary Africans, the low quality of education, the serious corruption and political instabilities in numerous states and many other debilitating failures. These challenges only point to a gloomy future for Africa if no change is made in the right direct to overcome Africa's ills.

Change

Which way for Africa? It appears that Africa has come full circle after independence to face the questions of change and choice again. In terms of what happens to Africa now, from our discussions so far suggest that the lack of clear vision and leadership has left Africa perilously exposed in a perpetually challenging world with no substantial capabilities to forcefully sustain the African people through difficult times. The changes that where promised by African leaders to their people, and for which many fought and paid the ultimate price with their lives never fully materialised.

Where do Africans go from here? This question throws up other questions concerning Africa's existence and development in the world. Has Africa been merely a dark, savage and mindless continent until the invasion of Arab and European forces? Were these Arab and European invaders the main forces of civilization in Africa? The answer to the latter as contentiously argued by the Pan-Africanist, John Henrik Clarke, is that no invading force that entered Africa brought with it any form of civilization other than exploitation and destruction. The significance of such an argument is evident in the struggle for survival and progress facing post-colonial Africa.

It could be argued that the introduction of Islam in Africa brought with it the skills of writing and reading among others. However, such an argument could be rejected on the basis of the prior existence of various forms of ancient writing systems in Africa before the onset of Arab invasion. What is clear, however, is that its destructive force in Africa remains and is demonstrated for example, in the rise of Boko-Haram, a brutal terrorist group in the Islamic heartlands of Nigeria that has brought mass abduction and sexual assault, death and wanton destruction of innocent people and property all in the name of defending and promoting Islam in Africa.

Similarly, the case could be made for the civilising effect of European domination in Africa in terms of its introduction of education and democracy. This too, could be refuted as African societies maintained sophisticated cultural and political systems before the arrival of the Europeans. The legacy of the European political structures injected into Africa can be observed in the enduring distortions that now exist within the African body politic. If the Europeans and Arabs were not wholly responsible for civilising Africans then we can contend that Africa was not simply a dark, savage and mindless continent before the arrival of foreign invaders. As already indicated, the impact of the curtailment and destruction of indigenous development in Africa by foreign intruders endures in the tenacious confusion associated with Africa's attempts to regain its authentic self.

It is possible to imagine how Africa could have been had she been uninterrupted in her development by foreign intruders. But is it achievable for Africans to attempt to reinstate a kind of pure African way of life based on fragmented historical recollections after centuries of colonial subjugation? To follow such line of thought may be extremely idealistic and impracticable in view of Africa's current set of circumstances. On the other hand, can Africans strive to regain and assemble where possible, helpful knowledge of their shattered pre-colonial past to retool their colonial experiences in order to shape a more positive future? This line of thinking could begin to answer the question concerning Africa's direction.

In order to shape a positive future, Africa must endeavour to simultaneously look back to ancient records to reaffirm her past successes, while moving forward by pragmatically blending the colonial experience with her ancient knowledge to build confidence in confronting the future. In the early heady era of independence, Africa faced the difficult task of choosing the right path for development when it won political freedom and proceeded through to the post-colonial era in chaotic transition. Leaders such as Nkrumah in Ghana and Nyerere in Tanzania chose African socialism while leaders like Houphouet-Boigny in the Ivory Coast resisted the socialist ideology. However, today in the twenty-first century, it still remains the case, arguably, that none of these African states can be hailed as free from their colonial crisis as poverty, inter-community rivalry and hindered development persist. Now with much hindsight, Africa can thoroughly and honestly reassess its position in relation to the development and wellbeing of Africans in order to make the right changes for a positive future.

As indicated earlier, the criticality of leadership for a positive African future cannot be overemphasised. The issues of incompetence and corruption that underline the chronic level of poor leadership at the core of the continuing mutilation of African development run deep. Such poor leadership possibly emanated from the pressure for 'Africanization' by the new post independence African elites that emerged to fill the positions of the skilled colonial administrators who were displaced at the end of the colonial era. For some of these African elites, independence became an end in itself that was achieved to lavishly reward them. In other words, independence came to mean taking the place of the colonial master to plunder and enjoy the privileges hitherto accorded to the colonial master.

Davidson's (1964) observation over half a century ago is interesting:

> For it is a fact, by and large (and generalization, one may perhaps repeat, will always be unfair to someone), that such 'leading elites' and 'middle classes' have largely collapsed under the strain of political independence. Some

have retired into profitable corruption, others into old-fashioned habits of colonial authoritarianism, still others into a more or less sterile defence of the status quo. For others, again, traditionalist separatism (we may call it, with reservation, tribalism) has become a major outlet for their energy. And given their often great authority among ordinary people, the example of these educated 'elites' and 'middle classes' has echoed down the ranks of African society with curious results (p131).

The incompetence and corruption of Africans 'on the make' in high administrative positions led Nkrumah of Ghana in a famous dawn broadcast to appeal for higher standards of morality while condemning luxury living and the personal dissipation of national wealth. In spite of his appeal for decency, such practices have endured through the decades to our present time, and freely demonstrated in the enjoyment of generous benefits including the use of super luxury vehicles by state serving African elites. In association with such immoral attitude is the insidious presence of 'tribalism' mentioned earlier, that is poisoning the teamwork needed for Africans to shape a positive future. Davidson (1964) again, had something interesting to say:

More often than some Africans care to admit, the coming of independence has meant a certain failure of nerve, a tendency to retreat within traditional enclosures, a search for new security inside an old amour of custom and belief (p136).

The irrefutable fact of conquest and its outcomes in Africa has left permanent marks regardless of how Africans would like to perceive these significant historical events. It is futile for Africans to seek new refuge in old customs and beliefs that failed to successfully resist subjugation and colonialism without any considerations for their inherent weaknesses. Answers to questions such as what made it possible for the successes of foreign incursions into Africa must include, among others, the African generosity extended to strangers on the one hand, and the latent rivalry between various African groups on the other hand. If there is any lesson that Africans and indeed all people of African decent can learn from the long period of their domination by foreign invaders is that of seeking cooperation by any means necessary to face the challenges of the future.   Although Africa's natural development was interrupted by foreign invasion, it inadvertently brought together diverse groups thus creating the possibility for the politically divided Africans to closely work together to tackle the problem of how to reconstruct a new society out of their colonial experiences.

Africa as already discussed, has had a very difficult period in charting a successful social and economic renewal since gaining political independence. What is presently clear is that Africans face an even greater struggle to reap the fruits of real emancipation as the political opportunities that presented themselves in the early days of independence have evolved into highly complex and entrenched positions that have undeniably come to hinder their prosperity.   Africans must renew their commitment and build up their courage to face the task of creating a new African society if they are to contribute to the shaping of the future world.

Building Confidence

At this juncture let us recall and examine the idea of linguistic unity proposed by Diop in our earlier discussion.   The interrelatedness of African languages provides a starting point for African cooperation. Sadly,

Diop's proposal for the use of an African language in an official continental capacity has failed to materialise, while regional languages continue to thrive on the local level. Diop's idea brings out the issue of who makes the choice and what measures should be used for such selection without alienating or offending users of lesser languages. Diop's suggestion that the task of choosing such an official language should be made by a knowledgeable 'interterritotrial commission' is reasonable, but it is not clear how such language once chosen can be effectively promoted.

For an African language to be embraced at high places in officialdom across the continent and by the African population it must exercise the appropriate cultural, economic and political power to dominate the spectrum of diverse but related African languages in ways that can only be described as benevolent linguistic imperialism. However, the most successful method that has resulted in the imposition of one group's language on another group has been through conquest, which no one group in Africa is in the position to do. Considering that no particular African language is as yet operating with such power as the English language is capable of exerting (Phillipson, 1992), it is therefore pragmatic for Africans to provisionally maintain the use of the English language and the other significant languages of the foreign forces that intervened in Africa namely, French and Arabic.

As part of the strategy to work towards the adoption of an official African language across the continent a concerted effort can be made to support Africans at local, national and continental levels to first gain some appreciation of the three foreign languages wherever possible. This effort could help strengthen confidence by the promotion of closer relationship and understanding between Africans. Considering that most Africans are multilingual should be an advantage in the adoption and learning of these languages. It must be understood that the suggestion being made here does not negate the desirability of a continental African language, but rather lays the basis for the introduction of such a language once discovered, agreed on and introduced to the people. Furthermore, the structural setup for the dissemination of the foreign languages could be used to provide a prepared path for the presentation and spread of the chosen African language, The choice of the language could be facilitated at the continental level by the African Union for delivery to the African people through the various member states. Using this approach therefore would mean that the officially accepted African language would also be used as the mode of communication simultaneously with the existing foreign languages until such time that the African language becomes fully established as the main medium of communication.

The teaching, learning, refinement and consolidation of the chosen African language could be managed at the state level by local universities and institutes on similar lines proposed by Nkrumah for the study of Africa at the University of Ghana, which was founded to undertake research into the Africa condition. Its foremost mission as expressed by Nkrumah in his opening speech was the need to re-interpret and reassess the factors that defined the African past through its history, culture, languages and arts, and to inspire the present and future generations with a vision of a better future. We will take a closer look at his speech later.

Nkrumah's underpinning idea for the institute still remains relevant and potent in promoting the rise of a continental African language. Such institutes with specific mission to promote African cultures focussed on the chosen continental language could be encouraged and supported by the African Union across the continent. The achievement of such a monumental task will directly depend on the willingness and competency of the African leadership to significantly and positively transform Africa through the collective desire and total devotion to a future in which Africans can thrive. The records show how Africa has not ceased to experience devastating failure since the beginning of the post-colonial era and it is now time for a fundamental change for the upliftment of the African people from their unremitting life of degradation for the majority.

Foresight

Developing the capacity for foresight is an important factor for Africa's future success. It will underpin the preparedness of Africans to face their myriad present and future problems. So far, the predominant mind-set in Africa is geared towards personal survival to the detriment of communal wellbeing. In other words, those in positions of power in Africa far too often fail to justly meet the monumental challenges of representing and working for the good of their own communities.

The issue of leadership discussed earlier cannot be overstated as the results of decades of African independence and self-government bear witness to the confusion and degradation across the continent. For the lack of leadership with foresight, Africa remains terrifyingly shackled to forces that may lead to its total neutering. As Kodjo (1989) poignantly observed:

> It will not emerge from the swamp of misery and dependency expect through colossal effort, by judiciously putting the forces of change into action, by breaking away from the mistaken ideas which, for a quarter of a century, have separated it from what seemed to be its natural vocation: the salt of the earth.

> Today, one is obliged to recognize that Africa barely exists. The media speak of it only to mention its conflicts, poverty, reveal its children with swollen bellies, and ribs sticking out, its cattle decimated by the drought, its people – more like sub-people – ravaged by hunger. From time to time, to complete the picture, a little religious war, a few ideological conflicts, a few massacres come along to put the finishing touches on the whole to give it an impression of non-being. In the public's mind, what exactly is Africa? A marginal entity, far away, backward, a sort of "terra incognita", incapable of managing it own affairs... (p3).

Decades after Kodjo's remarks significant improvements are yet to be clearly achieved in Africa. In other words, the lack of leadership and the colossal effort needed to transform Africa to its fitting station in the world remains a formidable challenge in the twenty-first century. The sorry state of Africa despite the continent's apparent progress guided the sharp commentary by Ayittey (2004):

> African leaders have failed Africa. African politicians have failed. African intellectuals have failed Africa, too. The failure is monumental and the international community is fed up with incessant African begging.

> Within a mere four decades after independence from colonial rule, Africa has been reduced to a broken, dysfunctional continent by wretched institutions and execrable leadership (p402).

Unless all Africans recognise and embrace the leadership challenges indicated in our earlier discussions, improving the current state of Africa and the wellbeing of all Africans can only remain beyond reach. It is arguable that today's Africa, where a democratic form of governance is still struggling to take genuine root after decades of military disruptions, is under mounting pressure driven by political leaders to distort the essence of democratic rule. Some leaders simply reject any notion of the transfer of power and rule until they pass away leaving their state to degenerate into disagreement and ultimately to civil war as in the case of the once prosperous state of Ivory Coast. The reluctance for the genuine transfer of political power has unfortunately become a prevalent narrative across much of the African continent as with increasing frequency some leaders are scheming to modify rules governing the transfer of power with the sole purpose of clinging on to power indefinitely and in some cases attempting to manoeuvre their family members into prominent positions to assume the reins of power after their demise. The lack of foresight and its damaging effect on African development as a consequence of poor leadership remains a formidable problem. Obviously, not everyone in a leadership position possesses the qualities and wisdom for leadership (Maathai, 2010). Yet, in Africa incompetence appears to be part of the stock-in-trade for political leadership.

Knowledge is arguably implicit in the elements of foresight for which, Havas[49] identifies five elements namely communication, concentration on the long term, consensus building, coordination and commitment to take actions as crucial factors in the development of foresight. Without the embrace of knowledge that

---

[49] See info at https://lei.hse.ru/en/news/119347850.html

entails an awareness of the past and a vision for the future, it is highly doubtful how a productive preparation for a brighter future can be achieved. In this regard, it is doubtful how Africans can face the future without committing to the truth in unity and the common purpose towards building a positive future for all Africans. The rejection of this fundamental knowledge is at the heart of the degradation facing the African world. The biblical story of the prophet Hosea crying out for his people perishing for lack of knowledge, in some way, captures the African predicament. The dire situation facing the African world is not borne out of ignorance but by the rejection of the truth in the notion of love and caring among Africans based on the knowledge of their shared experiences in the world. One may ask, why is Haiti still in a sorrowful state after more than two centuries of independence? Why do African Americans still form the majority at the bottom of the social ladder in a world they played a crucial role in creating? Why is Ghana, once a leader among nations and a shining beacon not only for African states but also for those far beyond its shores, now jaded with a blurred sense of purpose? While the usual easy answers tend to rest on slavery, colonialism and exploitation, Africans hardly want to take on the responsibility and the commitment of working together to create a better future. In the end, it is only Africans alone that can build a future that frees them from degradation. At this early stage in the twenty-first century, it is no longer a question of what do Africans do, but rather how committed are they in using the discovered fragments of their illustrious past and their painful experiences of the present to help shape a constructive future that is beneficial for all humanity in our perilous technological era.

Future Technology

How well will Africans thrive in the future considering their present standing in the world? A much broader question emerges in soliciting a response. Will the human race survive the twenty-first century? Rees (2003), a leading scientist was prompted to ask this question based on his assumption that our human civilization only has a 50% chance of surviving the new century due to the exhilarating rate at which science is advancing. Focussing on this century's present unfamiliar potential hazards that could threaten humanity and the entire global environment, Rees argues that our increasingly interconnected world is susceptible to new risks posed by biological or cyber development, or by intended terrorism or unintended error, and furthermore, the dangers from twenty-first century technology could be graver and more intractable than the threat of nuclear devastation that we faced for much of the twentieth century. Accordingly, human induced pressures on the global environment may engender higher risks than natural hazards such as earthquakes, volcanic eruption or asteroid impacts. Some of these threats Rees (2003) says, are already upon us and others are merely conjectural.

> Populations could be wiped out by lethal "engineered" airborne viruses; human character may be changed by new techniques far more targeted and effective than the nostrums and drugs familiar today; we may even one day be threatened by rogue nanomachines that replicate catastrophically, or by superintelligent computers.

> Other novel risks cannot be completely excluded. Experiments that crash atoms together with immense force could start a chain reaction that erodes everything on Earth; the experiments could even tear the fabric of space itself, an ultimate "doomsday" catastrophe whose fallout spreads at the speed of light to engulf the entire universe.

These latter scenarios may be exceedingly unlikely, but they raise in extreme form the issue of who should decide, and how, whether to proceed with experiments that have genuine scientific purpose (and could conceivably offer practical benefits), but that pose a very tiny risk of an utterly calamitous outcome (pp1–2).

The critical issue of who is qualified to make decisions on the supervision of scientific experiments with the potential to alter life as we know it, is presently highly likely to preclude Africa on the basis of its low scientific standing in spite of the increase in African scientific research output over the decades as reported by the World Bank[50]. Africa is yet to focus aggressively on the promotion of science, technology, engineering and mathematics as the most important areas for research and development, which can contribute significantly to the future development of Africa. For example, the continuing confusion regarding the impact of genetically modified organisms (GMOs) on African communities with particular reference to farming products[51] requires unbiased African scientific investigations to ascertain the true nature and implications for the introduction of such organisms into Africa. In the absence of African scientific resources to carry out such complex explorations, Africa faces a perilous future with regards to making the right choices in the face of powerful international organisations concerning the full-scale acceptance and use of GMOs. How strong will Africa be in the future to withstand the pressures from very powerful organisations such as the biotechnology giant Monsanto (Baird, 2015) to dominate and control food supply in Africa?

---

[50] See
http://documents.worldbank.org/curated/en/237371468204551128/pdf/9
10160WP0P126900disclose09026020140.pdf
[51] See Report in Guardian at https://www.theguardian.com/global-development/poverty-matters/2013/jun/24/gm-crops-african-farmers

Managing Power

Without the power to fully account for, and exercise control over key possessions such as human and natural resources, Africa risks the grave danger of reaching a new low in becoming totally insignificant in the world and as a consequence could ultimately end up in an unimaginable level of subjugation and degradation. The undeniable problem for Africa in the twenty-first century is the establishment of power that cares for justice.

What does it mean to be powerless? If the answer relates to the absence of power then let us begin by considering the nature of power. Although the idea of power is firmly embedded in everyday language usage it is surprisingly not so easy to ascertain how one entity is more powerful than another. Exploring from a social perspective, Russell (2004) described power as the production of intended effects, and consequently it could be viewed as a quantitative concept. However, Russell argued that there is no exact means of comparing the power of two individuals X and Y who are able to achieve their sets of different desires. For example, given two drivers of whom each wishes to drive from Johannesburg to Maputo and participate in an annual arts festival, and one succeeds in driving to Maputo and the other in participating in the arts festival, in this case there is no way of estimating which has the more power. Conversely, according to Russell, it is not difficult to say, generally, that X has more power than Y, if X achieves many intended effects and Y only a few. Like the notion of love which most of us acknowledge to be important, we experience power in diverse ways in our everyday lives with real effects notwithstanding our incapability to precisely measure it.

The concept of power can be classified in various ways such as power over human beings or power over non-human forms of life made possible by the advancement of science, and each with its own usefulness. Focusing on the power over human beings, it may be further classified by the manner of influencing individuals or by the type of organisation involved. For example, an individual may be influenced by direct physical power over his or her body, or by rewards and inducements, or by influencing opinion through propaganda and drill. These forms of power are most explicitly displayed in our dealing with animals where pretences and disguises are stripped away. For example when a goat secured by a rope is lifted into a holding pen, it is subject to direct physical power over its body. On the other hand, when fresh cut grass is used to entice the goat it is induced to do so by persuasion, a conditioning out of which habits can be formed based on rewards and punishments. In a different way, sheep induced into a holding pen when the leader has to be dragged in by force, and the rest then willingly follow. For Russell, all these forms of power are exemplified among human beings. The case of the goat being handled into the pen illustrates military and police power. The goat with the grass symbolises the power of propaganda and education. The sheep following their grudging leader represent organised or party politics wherever a leader is in bondage to a clique or party controllers.

Hence the most important organisations are approximately distinguishable by the kind of power that they exert. The army and the police exercise coercive power over the body whereas economic organisations display their power using rewards and punishments as incentives and deterrents, meanwhile schools, religious groups and political parties focus on influencing opinion. The state as an organisation expresses power in its ultimate and coercive use of the law, a set of rules according to which the state maintains its privilege in dealing with its citizens. However, the law is almost powerless when it is not supported by public sentiment, which illustrates the difference between newly acquired or revolutionary power and traditional power.

The force of habit developed through respect that requires no continual justification nor proof that it faces formidable opposition seeking to overthrow it is what underpins traditional power, which is mostly associated with religious or quasi-religious beliefs and can rely on public opinion to a greater extent than revolutionary or usurped power. Since traditional power feels secure it does not seek out traitors and political tyranny is mostly avoided. However, where ancient institutions persist, the injustices to which agents of power are always prone have the permission of ancient custom and consequently can be more obvious than would be possible under a new form of government looking for popular support.

Russell termed power not based on tradition as "naked" power, and went further to make important distinctions between traditional, revolutionary and naked power. Traditional power is not merely due to its ancient form but must also command respect borne partly out of custom. Revolutionary power arises when a large group is united by a new creed, programme or sentiment. Naked power results simply from the power-loving impulses of individuals or groups, which is usually military and may take the form either of internal tyranny or foreign conquest, which wins from its masses only submission through fear and not active collaboration.

Russell's work gives us some insight into the nature of power. However, some commentators disagree with Russell on his thesis that the love of power is a basic human motive, as power constitutes the fundamental concept in social science similar to the way in which energy is the fundamental concept in physics.

Nye (2011) says the comparison is misleading as the relations of energy and force among inanimate objects in physics can be precisely measured, whereas power in the social setting refers to more ephemeral human relationships based on varying circumstances. However, Russell's analysis anticipated what is now called cyberpower by his consideration of human power over non-human forms of existence through the application of science. Although power based on information is not new Nye argues that cyberpower is new in his consideration of the future of power in the affairs of the world.

Focusing on the United States, currently the undisputed military superpower in the twenty-first century, Nye examines what it means to be powerful today and for the United States to remain at the apex of power it must adopt a strategy that considers the impact of the internet on power resources across the world. By this perspective power resources firstly consist of the tangible and intangible raw materials, or vehicles that underpin power relationships and secondly, the extent to which a given set of resources produces preferred outcomes or not depends on the behaviour in context. In other words, power can be defined in terms of resources and also as behavioural outcomes. However, in both cases it is the achievement of the preferred outcome that signifies power. Considering tangible resources for example, since technologies have evolved and proliferated over the century changes in the sources of military strength no longer make war the final arbitrator.

Nye argues that strategies that relate means to ends provide a critical variable and those that combine tangible and intangible resources successfully in different contexts to produce preferred outcomes are the key to what he called smart power. Nye's discussion of the future distribution of power among the industrial states in the world with particular reference to the United States and China subtly underline Africa's apparent weakness in influencing world affairs.

The development and organisation of power that is required for Africa to emerge as a force is yet to be realised in spite of its resource assets. It is tragic that the economic foundation for the development of power that was well understood by Nkrumah in his political struggle for African unity and common purpose remains largely misunderstood by significant African leaders. How is it possible for Africa to fully flourish in the foreseeable future without seeking the capacity to determine its own way? What will be the fate of Africans in a future world without their presence among the powerful in the world? Arguably, one of the underlying factors that gave rise to the exploitation and abuse of Africans for centuries may be attributed to their lack of control over circumstances directly affecting them as already indicated by Williams (1987). In a future world where competition for resources is very likely to grow even fiercer as a result of increasing demands by various states and non-state actors, basic human and environmental pressures and increasing scarcity of resources, it is not difficult to envisage how the conditions of Africans can only get worse if they continue to fail to exert any kind of power on a future world stage. In short, it would be almost impossible for Africa to fully flourish in the foreseeable future without the ability to determine its own direction of development amidst the tensions and growing redistribution of economic, political and military power in the world.

The struggles by some of the political figures in the African world have been underpinned by their understanding of the critical nature of economic success in the organisation and maintenance of power. The distinguished African American educator and author Booker T. Washington advocated the development of economic power for African Americans. Born into slavery, Washington became the leading voice of former slaves and their descendants and called for African American progress through education and entrepreneurship as the path to power, rather than directly challenging the political system of the era. He mobilised a coalition of African American leaders and other sympathetic American supporters with a long-term plan of building the economic strength and pride of the African American community by a focus on self-reliance.

In *Up From Slavery*, Washington (1986) clearly articulated his vision for the empowerment of the African American in a keynote speech given to the National Education Association:

> [T]he future of the Negro rested largely upon the question as to whether or not he should make himself, through his skill, intelligence, and character, of such undeniable value to

the community in which he lived that the community could
not dispense with his presence (p 202).

For Washington:

[A]ny individual who learned to do something better than
anybody else – learned to do a common thing in an
uncommon manner – had solved his problem, regardless of
the colour of his skin, and that in proportion as the Negro
learned to produce what other people wanted and must
have, in the same proportion would he be respected (p202).

These thoughts formed the basis for the path that
Washington took towards the real emancipation of the
African American from the ravages of slavery.
Washington's philosophy and its dissemination meant
that he had to thread a fine line at this stage in American
history in simultaneously satisfying three different
groups, namely the northern white Americans who
opposed slavery and its attendant ramifications on the
one hand, and the southern white Americans resistant to
any concession to their grip on slavery and the related
power that it generates through social and economic
avenues on the other hand and more significantly, the
devastated   African   American   community   he
represented.   Washington's   position   involved
compromises that had to be made. He urged African
Americans   as   a   temporary   measure   to   accept
discrimination and concentrate on elevating themselves
through hard work and material prosperity, elements he
considered to be the sure foundation for their future
acceptance and recognition as equal citizens in all strata
of society.

The farsightedness of Washington in encouraging the
newly freed African slaves in America to develop their
economic power, however, did not spread unchallenged
and the result somehow has continued to affect the

African world. The voice that rose the highest in presenting a different view was that of W.E.B. Dubois, one of the most illustrious African American intellectuals. In contrast to Washington who largely funded his own education, Dubois came from a relatively secure family background and gained his educational qualifications from some of the finest institutions in America and Europe. Dubois's position was that Washington's strategy would serve only to perpetuate the oppression of African Americans. For Dubois political action and a civil rights agenda must be the vanguard for the emancipation of the African American. Although Dubois acknowledged Washington for his unceasing effort to help alleviate the suffering of African Americans, he roundly criticised him for the possible implications of his approach. For Dubois, Washington arose essentially as a leader connecting various communities, a compromiser between the South, the North and the African American and thus becoming manifest in African American thought the old attitude of adjustment and submission. In his seminal book *The Souls of Black Folk*, Dubois (1989) made a forceful case:

> Mr. Washington's programme practically accepts the alleged inferiority of the Negro races. Again, in our land, the reaction from the sentiment of wartime has given impetus to race-prejudice against Negroes, and Mr Washington withdraws many of the high demands of Negroes as men and American citizens. In other periods of intensified prejudice all the Negro's tendency to self-assertion has been called forth; at this period a policy of submission is advocated. In the history of nearly all races and peoples the doctrine preached at such crises has been that manly self-respect is worth more than lands and houses, and that a people who voluntarily surrender such respect, or cease striving for it, are not worth civilizing (p43).

He continued:

In answer to this, it has been claimed that the Negro can survive only through submission. Mr Washington distinctly asked that black people give up, at least for the present, three things, –

First, political power,

Second, insistence on civil rights,

Third, higher education of the Negro, –

And concentrate all their energies on industrial education, the accumulation of wealth and the conciliation of the South (p44).

Then concluded:

As a result of this tender of the palm-branch, what has been the return? In these years there have occurred:

1. The disenfranchisement of the Negro
2. The legal creation of a distinct status of civil inferiority for the Negro
3. The steady withdrawal of aid from institutions for the higher training of the Negro (p44).

Washington's propaganda, according to Dubois contributed significantly to the facilitation of the above results. For Dubois (1903) social change could be attained by the development of a small group of college educated African Americans that he referred to as "the Talented Tenth" to lead:

The Negro Race, like all races, is going to be saved by its exceptional men. The problem of education then, among Negroes, must first of all deal with the Talented Tenth; it is the problem of developing the Best of this race that they may guide the Mass away from the contamination and death of the worst in their own and other races. Now the training of men is a difficult and intricate task. Its technique is a matter for educational experts, but its object is for the vision of seers. If we make money the object of man-training, we shall develop money-makers but not necessarily men; if we make technical skill the object of education, we may possess artisans but not, in nature, men. Men we shall have only as we make manhood the object of the work of the schools- intelligence, broad sympathy,

knowledge of the world that was and is, and of the relation
of men to it - this is the curriculum of that Higher Education
which must underlie true life. On this foundation we may
build bread winning, skill of hand and quickness of brain,
with never a fear lest the child and man mistake the means
of living for the object of life (pp33-34).

The difference in viewpoints at the time between
Washington and Dubois divided African American
leaders into two factions, the so-called 'conservative'
supporters of Washington and his 'radical' opponents.
While the controversy between Washington and Dubois
may appear irreconcilable John Henrik Clarke held that
both positions are fundamentally relevant in the
struggle for the upliftment of the African people.
However, the Dubois philosophy of agitation and protest
for civil rights streamed directly into the development of
the Civil Rights movement in preference to the
restrained approach of Washington.

After a century of struggle for freedom and power by
people of African descent in the world how may we
summarise their progress? Clearly much progress has
been made concerning civil rights and political
independence across the African world but these gains
have not fully translated to highly successful economic
independence and prosperity. In retrospect, could it be
possible to argue that Washington's message seems to
be relevant in the post-colonial and post-racial world of
the twenty-first century?

In the last century the African world has produced
powerful political leaders such as Garvey and Nkrumah
who attempted to restore the dignity of their people.
However, their painful struggle has long lost its practical
meaning in terms of the inadequate gains made toward
their general prosperity and wellbeing. This situation is

arguably exemplified by the debilitating conditions still existing in the African world today.

There is much heated debate as to why the African world remains trapped in poverty and degradation in spite of the gains made for political power. An element that refuses to subside throughout this debate is the issue of unity for economic empowerment and wellbeing. This has always been at the centre of the rallying call by all the great leaders of the African world, a call that is yet to be fully heeded. In his historical work on the destruction of African civilisation, Williams (1987) could not be clearer:

> For the Black world, history's Watchman could see no sign of promise, no sign of hope outside of a position of strength which unity alone can provide. But there will never be a real unity without a *plan* and a *program* to sustain it. Petty power struggles, bickering and attacking each other are all signs of a death wish as a race. "Which way, then, you still shackled Blacks?" Six thousand years of their history has answered: Unite or perish. The tragedy that bloodied the pages in every period of their history because of disunity should be warning enough for the Blacks of Africa, the Caribbean, and elsewhere. But being the one people who are generally ignorant of their history, it may well be that many will not see unity as a question of life and death. However, there has been so much history during the time of those now living that the precarious situation of the black race should be obvious to all. Only a largely united people can successfully confront oppressors and, without praying on bended knees, or even pleading, secure the removal of all shackling chains. The choice is between unity of action in calm, careful thinking and planning the course of action through one vast organisation of millions – either this or ultimate damnation. If the race is incapable of unity, it is incapable of survival as a free and equal people, and will deserve all the iniquities imposed upon it, for it will have proved beyond all question that it is indeed unfit to survive as a people free and equal in every respect whatsoever with the other peoples of the world (pp32–326).

Williams then points out the situation in a reflective mood:

> How long the black race will stand at the crossroads,
> uncertain what to do, confused, and, in fact actually afraid,
> how long, only future history will tell (p328).

The sustained length and depth of the brutal degradation that went into the creation of the existing confusion among Africans in the world has produced a monumental task, one that will in no doubt require intergenerational thinking and planning for any hopeful prospect in combating current difficult conditions. Williams recognises the importance of economic power as the basis for any meaningful progress and argues that for the African people who are most victimised everywhere, their own situation can be changed radically in a cooperative programme. However, such a cooperative must be fundamentally different in its aims and objectives that include, but go beyond mere economic cooperatives toward a more compassionate economic system that can allow for the promotion of genuine positive development. Williams presents a provisional master plan with a particular focus on African Americans to provide the lead for unity in the African world. The plan is structured around various important activities that consist of the following divisions: Economic Planning and Development, Political Action, Public Education, Community Services, Youth Activities, Pan African Affairs, Intelligence and Security. Williams also proposes a Commission for Spiritual Life and Assurance:

> (1) to determine the direction of civilization; (2) to
> interpret the "spiritual" as men and women working on the
> highest level of humane endeavors to understand the

meaning of life while trying to improve it; (3) to enlist the cooperation of white, brown, yellow and red and any and all other peoples od goodwill in an all-out drive to for a better world; (4) to maintain an emergency assistance program for families or communities in distress; (5) and to assume the initiative in seeking the active cooperation of any and all religious faiths and all institutions which are concerned with improving human relations and, therefore, life itself (p355).

Williams sees the development of a movement from his master plan that can assist the African people to begin to learn the futility of grasping as their own, unsuitable ideologies such as capitalism or socialism not specifically designed for their upliftment. He urges them to focus on developing their own solutions based on an ideology operating within the framework of the traditional African philosophy of life and the best of its value system.

The exploratory ideas offered by Williams in his master plan proposals in some ways resonate with the work of Anderson (2001) in his national plan to lead African Americans in particular, and in general the oppressed Africans in the world to political and economic self-sufficiency and competitiveness. The central idea in Anderson's plan involves the importance of having group self-interest and a sense of group competition in ways that are in their own best interest.   Anderson maintains that it is utterly futile for African Americans to march and protest for civil rights and equality when they have no economic base for political leverage. On this issue, Anderson clearly validates Washington's argument made over a century ago that the newly freed African slaves in America must first focus on developing a strong economic base through the mastery of trades vital to their communities which will in time positively impact their fight for political power.   Anderson structures his plan on five levels beginning with (1) a new economic model for building wealth through the practice of group economics within the African American neighbourhoods (2) how African Americans can use their economic power to demand political power; (3) bring their economic voice to bear on policing, the courts and the justice system; (4) control the media; (5) influence education.

African Americans, from Anderson's perspective, cannot successfully compete in the American system because they possess nothing, and for the large part of their existence they are merely consumers that produce nothing in return. In other words, their survival is highly at risk, as they control nothing. Without unity to compete as an economic group, Anderson argues, in a very similar manner as Williams, Nkrumah and Garvey did before him that people of African descent in the world are in danger of total irrelevance if present conditions and level of disunity persist. In all the various calls and explanations for African unity and renewal education remains at the core of such appeals, but what kind of education is most appropriate for the people of African descent in our present world to employ in shaping a better future?

Education

Certainly, education in its broadest sense is a critical component among other key elements in the preservation and transmission of culture, and in doing so it must function as a system for fashioning survival techniques and development tools for various communities. But how does a group of people who have lost all or a greater part of their history and are only likely to regain a minor portion of what could be retrieved engage in education relevant for their future wellbeing? The unique history of the African people is one that belongs to all humanity. As a people autochthonous to Africa with reasonable evidence pointing to the African continent as the birthplace of humanity, which suggests an African link to human development and civilisation, what kind of future lies ahead for the people of African descent?

After centuries of oppression, the unfortunate impact of the painful history of the African people and their descendants in the world indicates that a system of education to help them address their issues remains to be fully realised. The demise of the great ancient African civilisations brought with it a history told by the conquerors of the supposed backwardness of the African people, and in order to sustain such narratives devised fitting curricula that have not only persisted for centuries but have also contributed to lasting damaging effects on humanity in general and the African people in particular.

Pre-colonial Education

The dark ages for Africans started well over two thousand years ago (Williams, 1987), a time so distant in the past that has allowed generations of Africans and non-Africans to be taught to believe Africans were savages who never came out of the darkness until the arrival of the conquering Arabs and Europeans brought civilisation to them. The tragic loss of important pieces of knowledge missing from the pages of African history have left the people of African descent vulnerable to accepting questionable but deeply rooted non-African historical narratives that have survived through the centuries to our present time. Much has been written on traditional African education for which some commentators (Tedla, 1992) have attempted to provide a comprehensive account spanning thousands of years while others (deGraft Johnson, 1956; Boateng, 1983; Omolewa, 2007) have merely provided outlines of such traditional education. Arguably, the difficulties in ascertaining the beginnings of educational systems in Africa could be related firstly, to the very ancient nature of the African people reaching back into the remotest and unreachable collective memory of humanity and secondly, to the persistent domination and degradation of African life through ceaseless wars and occupations by external and internal invaders over the ages, culminating in the present confused state of Africa facilitated by the Arab and European conquest of the continent.

In obliterating much of what was left of the past memory of African forms of passing on knowledge and history in general, the invading Arabs and Europeans in the first instance spread their worldview in Africa mainly though religion, consequently the initial form of education they brought to the native African was focused on religious indoctrination. European domination and later colonisation of Africa, which subsequently impeded the spread of Islam across the continent, advanced its control by the selective training and engagement of members of the African community useful to the European mission.

Colonial Education

The movement of Europeans along the Western coast of Africa for trade was the period in history that led to the production of the first African to be ordained a minister of the Church of England; the life story of Philip Quaque (1741- 1816) is interesting. Born at Cape Coast (in present-day Ghana), Quaque was still a child when Rev. Thomas Thompson was sent to Cape Coast by the Society for the Propagation of the Gospel (SPG) in 1751 as the first Anglican missionary in Africa. However, after five years sojourn and very little progress made in converting the Africans Thompson concluded that success in the propagation of the gospel could only be attained if native Africans were educated and trained to preach to their own people. Quaque, whose father was a local chief and had very cordial relationship with the English agreed for his son to be recommended by Thompson for this purpose and sent to England in 1754 at the expense of the SPG. After his baptism in 1759 as Philip Quaque, he was ordained as a minister in 1766 and in the following year returned to Cape Coast Castle as a chaplain. By the time of Quaque's arrival at Cape Coast there was no trace of the school that Thompson attempted to set up a decade earlier to propagate the gospel (Bartels, 1955). However, repeated requests made to Quaque by his fellow Africans for a school soon after his arrival encouraged him to open one in 1766 with the support of his English superiors. The content of the curriculum as expected was simple; it consisted of religious instruction with the aid of the church catechism to instil Christian principles. Reading lessons were provided by the alphabetic spelling method, which were offered though primers and spelling books provided by the SPG for the purpose. The principal reading book was the catechism itself. The art of writing was introduced later when the pupils gained proficiency in reading. Quaque's endeavours met with various challenges throughout his entire service as a missionary and teacher until his death in 1816, however, his work was among the pioneering efforts that went into the eventual provision of colonial education in Africa. Remarkably, the school Quaque founded has remained in existence to our present time and it is very interesting to reflect on its role on the promotion of education for the local people and the changes that it had experienced through the centuries.

At the onset of European colonial involvement in Africa, in addition to spreading the gospel through the teaching of reading and writing that underpinned much of the work of Quaque, the need for African clerks able to read, write, keep accounts and act as mediators between European traders and their African counterparts led to the development and expansion of local education to mitigate the cost of educating suitable Africans in Europe. While much of such earlier European education was privately provided by missionary, charitable or merchant societies the move from private to public provision was a slow one. One must bear in mind that at the time of Quaque's effort to promote education at Cape Coast the slave trade was an accepted, widespread and above all very lucrative business and Cape Coast was a major slave trading centre among other trading businesses that were carried out there between the Africans and Europeans.

Attempts to relocate African slaves taken to the New World as part of the effort to address the issues of slavery led to the settlement of Freetown in 1792 and the formation of the colony of Sierra Leone. The development of the population of Sierra Leone as a unique composition of displaced Africans who were brought to the colony after the British abolition of the slave trade in 1807. Freetown served as the colonial residence of the British governor who also administered the Gold Coast (Ghana) and Gambia settlements. Due to its centrality, Sierra Leone developed as the educational hub of British West Africa leading to the establishment of Fourah Bay College in 1827 by the Church Missionary Society of the Anglican Church for the training of teachers and missionaries to serve in the promotion of education and Christianity in West Africa. For more than a century the college represented the only European type institution of higher learning in Western Africa, which gave Africans training and positions in the colonial administration across the region.

The Berlin Conference of 1884 marked the climax of European competition in Africa, a situation that arguably generated new interest in Africa for the consolidation of old territories and push for new ones with the intention of securing needed natural resources. This renewed interest may have had some impact on education and training of Africans by their colonial overlords for the purpose of assisting with the administration and exploitation of these territories more formally. The nineteenth century witnessed the beginnings of formal education for Africans provided by the European powers and similarly for the descendants of African slaves in America by Christian charitable means as exemplified by the African Institute (now known as Cheyney University of Pennsylvania), the oldest African American institution of higher learning established in 1837 by Richard Humphreys[52], a Quaker philanthropist to educate and prepare descendants of Africans in America as teachers

---

[52] See info at
http://www.swarthmore.edu/Library/friends/ead/4059rihu.xml

in the various branches of trades. Meanwhile, on the African continent the initial formal development of education by the European powers reflected their imperialist plans.

The British for example, were interested in adopting efficient ways to manage their colonies and subsequently encouraged Christian missionary societies to provide education cheaply on their behalf. These missionaries had considerable freedom in how they operated their schools, how they recruited their teachers and taught religion. They were also free to adjust their curriculum to suit local conditions, which made their educational system largely decentralised. Furthermore, the English language was used in addition to local languages as the medium of instruction.

For the French however, education was key to turning Africans into Frenchmen and to this end they applied the ideology of assimilation in their African educational provision. Consequently, schools were unable to function without government permission and were controlled by a government prescribed curriculum, which was delivered by government-certified teachers using the French language as the only medium of instruction. The churches were prohibited from playing any significant role thus leaving the state to exclusively bear the cost of providing education for their colonies (Garnier and Schafer 2006).

The Germans on the other hand approached the provision of education in their African colonies differently than both the French and British. The German colonial administration was less interested in transforming the African into a German but rather interested in having an African capable of understanding the German definition of work (vanderPleog, 1977). In other words, the German interest in educating Africans was driven purely by economic interest, which required the need for literate and numerate Africans capable of fulfilling their work obligations through the use of the German language. In pursuing this aim the Germans also used their Christian missionaries of Basel to promote education in Africa that offered the opportunity to become a teacher, a clerk, a printer, an interpreter or a carpenter for example, these trades offered a new employment structure.

The three different educational systems employed by the Europeans all contributed to the exploitation of the natural and human resources in Africa which continued until the outbreak of the First World War in 1914, which led directly to the loss of Germany's African colonies to Britain and France, the victors in 1918. The impact of the war on Africa was devastating due to the death of approximately one million Africans[53] from various parts of the colonies who died in East Africa while assisting their colonial masters in the fight. It also led to the production of larger numbers of educated Africans to help increase productivity for the replenishment of the colonial economy after the war. Serious considerations regarding the position of the Africans began to surface as presented by the Governor of the Gold Coast at the time, Sir Frederick Guggisberg (1922). The chief duty of the Government, according to Guggisberg:

> It is nothing more nor less than assisting the Native Races of the Country in their progress towards the attainment of those conditions in their progress of modern civilisation which are best suited to the country (pp81–82).

---

[53] See info at http://www.dw.com/en/africa-and-the-first-world-war/a-17573462

Guggisberg took part in the war before retuning to Gold Coast, an experience that may have given him a fresh and deeper perspective on the responsibilities of the Colonial government towards its colonies especially in the provision of the resources for education. He argued that:

> The chief element in progress is education- education of the right sort- education in its wider sense. Not merely education in letters, mathematics, sciences- education in character- moral education in such directions as will develop good citizens- in fact, education that will eventually place the Native Races on an equality with the European Nations with which they must inevitably contend in the World's struggle for existence (p82).

Guggisberg was very insightful in identifying some shortcomings of colonial education in its curriculum focus on promoting only literary education at the expense of handwork or practical education this is a point that incidentally highlights some of the good aspects of the German system in providing a sort of technical education, Guggisberg even admits that the severest blow dealt by the war to Africa is the withdrawal of the Basel Mission as a result of the German defeat. Furthermore, he highlights the absence of an important aspect of British education missing in the African system namely the building of efficient character training. Guggisberg's proposals were far reaching in their intentions for expanding primary education to address the growing population, followed by technical training institutions, teacher training colleges and a medical school. These proposals arguably came to underpin the agenda for national development when the Gold Coast became the first colony in Africa to gain independence.

Postcolonial Education

By the mid twentieth century the impact of the Second World War had contributed to the demand for independence across the African colonies, which culminated in the emergence of political freedom in Africa. The Gold Coast was renamed Ghana by its new African leaders on the eve of independence in 1957 and immediately faced the task of national development. A key factor at the dawn of freedom for the newly independent colonies hinged on the availability of relevant human resource, in other words, a well-trained and competent workforce to drive forward the development needed to lift up the colonies from centuries of dependency. Guggisberg forestalled this development problem much earlier and his efforts to address the problem led to the founding of educational institutions in Ghana that formed the basis upon which leaders of the independence movement emerged. The two main educational issues that faced Africans at the onset of the postcolonial era were firstly, the need to increase the educational provision for citizens in order to eliminate illiteracy and secondly, how to remodel the educational experience to fall in line with the central goals for national development.

The criticality of having a literate and numerate population for the transformation of dependant colonies to independent African states was understood by African independence leaders who made it a key part of their struggle for freedom, however, the achievement of this goal has eluded African states since their bid for independence. Stated in a United Nations Monitoring Report[54] despite progress in access to schooling the

---

[54] View report at
http://unesdoc.unesco.org/images/0023/002322/232205e.pdf

dropout rate remains an issue in Africa given that a significant number of children enrolled in primary education are not expected to reach the last grade. Furthermore, in terms of gender equality the poorest girls remain the most likely to never attend primary school.   According to the report Africa records the highest illiteracy rate among adults.

Evidently, the beginnings of educational provision for Africans throughout the colonial period were based on European models, and these systems have endured through their indelible marks left on African education. In an address to the Royal Society of Arts in England by a key founding member of the Prince of Wales College at Achimota in contemporary Ghana, Rev. A.G. Fraser (1933) presented a detailed outline of the formation and progress of the institution which emerged from Governor Guggisberg's (1922) education reform programme that defined and laid the foundation and subsequent benchmark for education through the formative years of the postcolonial period in Africa. Prince of Wales College began as a boarding secondary school for boys where technical skills could be developed alongside the training of teachers. It is interesting to note that in 1922 a technical school was established by the British in East Africa that evolved into Makerere University Uganda. The far sightedness of the Prince of Wales College project led by Rev Fraser was different in that it quickly expanded to include the education of girls and primary aged children as well extending its sphere to include the provision of higher education as the college developed.   Consequently, the long-term remit of the college came to cover the entire learning experience.

The lower primary and kindergarten school sector of the College introduced their pupils to learning using the four main vernacular languages spoken in Ghana namely Ewe, Ga, Fanti and Twi as the medium of instruction. Fraser justified the use of the languages in its helpfulness in increasing the interest of the pupils in the foundations of their subjects including arithmetic, geography, history, oral composition, etc. Fraser maintained that the use of the vernaculars gave the pupils a more rapid advance through the lower primary classes and furthermore it helped them to learn English and its pronunciation much better thus giving them a solid foundation in the upper years where the English language was used as the medium of instruction. We will later discuss in more detail the attempt to provide education fully from an African perspective. Throughout the Prince of Wales College and school all pupils are taught to take an interest in agriculture, beginning with little flower gardens to vegetables and livestock work involving cattle, poultry, etc. All its pupils study some science, some agriculture,, some handicraft, some art, some music and some woodcarving, furthermore, it provided English degrees in engineering, science and arts. The breadth and depth of the education offered at the College meant that pupils who started at the kindergarten stage could stay for fourteen years before leaving. The educational experience envisioned for the college highlighted the development of a fecund frame of mind for the acceptance of responsibility by graduates of the institution in their eventual profession capacities. This vision was in no doubt set to raise the African beyond the mere gaining of vocational skills as it was in the early stages of education provided by Europeans for Africans. Fraser (1933) provided a clear idea of this type of education:

In the early days of the colonies the desire that children should be educated lay largely with the European, whether administrator, merchant or missionary. The first need in their minds was to find clerks, interpreters, catechists and subordinate officials, and schools were directed to supply this want. The schools were literary but vocational, and very soon their products filled the vocations for which they were trained, and there was left a surplus for whom no place could be found (p817).

He then went on to say:

A predominantly vocational system of education can hardly fail to be dangerous, for its outlets are not as wide as the needs of a nation. We are sometimes told that the solution of all African educational problems is to be found in vocational education. But the reason of the disillusionment in regard to past education is that it was overwhelmingly vocational and too soon filled up the vocations catered for. The real work for education was sacrificed to narrow vocational ends (p817).

Although Fraser was not explicit in providing the source for his comment on vocational education being the solution for Africa's educational problems, the idea had gained much traction and acceptability through the work done at Tuskegee Institute by Booker T. Washington for Africans emerging from slavery in the late nineteenth century America.

Fraser's argument for African education in some way resonated with the position taken by W.E.B. Dubois in expressing a different position to the view held by Washington regarding vocational education.

For Fraser:

The immediate aim of African education should be to develop the character, initiative, independence and ability of her youth, so that they may be reliable, courageous, and intelligent in the rapidly changing life and circumstances of their own people. The aim is to enrich the lives of the young for the sake of their own peoples. Our College prayer ends thus: "Bless Thou this place and may Thy glory dwell herein. May its sons and daughters come to know the life that is life indeed, and go forth from it as living waters to a thirsty land."

The first essential towards this aim of imparting life is to create an atmosphere of freedom (p817).

Fraser's aim for African education is still relevant in the twenty-first century considering the present state of the African continent. His faith in Africans and concern for their success cannot be denied:

> I am not fearful that the good things of Africa shall be lost. The African peoples are virile and are in their own continent where strangers must always be comparatively few. Therefore, as far as I can see, our main business is to impart so far as in us lies an understanding of western civilisation, together with an appreciation of the African background. Our students should be to understand policies, politics and problems thrown up continuously by the clash of old and new. To be qualified to modify a people's historical achievement or civilisation men must be not only conversant with it but in sympathy with it. We require and must aim at the will to work, readiness to take responsibility, and a developed capacity to think clearly and to act resolutely. To educate men capable of great leadership means the united thought of African and European working together. They must know each other and be frank with one another, all cards on the table. We have an immense opportunity before us. Unlike the case of Europe, our educational system is starting before the State, and it will be creative of the State, as European education never had the chance to be (p819).

As his contribution to the preparation of Africans for independence the commitment that Fraser brought to the education project is supreme particularly in his endeavour to blend aspects of African culture with European civilisation. The justification for moving in such a direction is implicit in the centuries old intimate relationship between Africa and Europe. Although the model championed by Fraser came to dominate in Africa, the opportunity to explore the viability of wholly indigenous education was not missed. For example, the Malangali School project was a limited experiment started from about 1928 to around 1933 in present day Tanzania, proposed by W.B. Mumford (1930) to base the education of Africans wholly on tribal institutions but interwoven with portions of European culture. Such an educational experiment developed from the compromise between cultural assimilation and adaptation (Iliffe, 1994) but more slanted towards the latter, which, at its simplest, often meant organising a school's pupil allocation in terms of houses based on tribal orientations.

For the French as already shown, the idea of assimilation was the goal in their educational provision throughout their African colonies (Cogneau and Moradi, 2014)[55]. Education in the French colonies for the reformation of the African to cherish French values was encouraged through the exclusive use of French as the language of instruction. Before the advent of independence French colonial education was controlled by the government, particularly concerning the establishment of a new school, the engagement of teachers and the curriculum to follow. According to White (1996):

> There are three features which can be said to characterise French colonial education in sub-Saharan Africa. First is the widespread use of the French language. There were scattered unsuccessful experiments with local languages and France would later permit the short-term use of African

---

[55] See article at http://voxeu.org/article/british-and-french-educational-legacies-africa

languages in order to meet 'immediate' pedagogical needs such as health education and morality, but all instruction had the mastery of the French language as its ultimate goal. Second is the enrolment limitation, which was based on estimates of job availability for graduating students. By implementing this policy of educational supply and demand, the French Government hoped to prevent the disillusion and disorientation experienced by youths who were educated but unemployed. Third is the dual nature of the French colonial school system. African schools were intended to educate the masses. European schools, on the other hand, were more selective and were concerned with educating an African elite that could eventually fill the lower ranks of the colonial civil service (pp11-12).

The French educational system contributed in some ways to the pre-independence resistance in the African colonies, which for many came to symbolise political and cultural domination. As White (1996) concluded, many Africans viewed the rural education programmes with its emphasis on agriculture and crafts training as a hidden attempt to keep Africans uneducated and powerless. The highly selective French schools on the other hand were seen as elitist and insufficient.

In contrast to the French, the British government's involvement in formal education in Africa was much less visible as activities by other agencies such as missionaries were encouraged in their provision of education for the Africans. The legacy of the French and British educational systems at the beginning of the postcolonial period in Africa showed some differences and indeed shared some similarities. The key differences between the two colonial powers is linked to the nature of their political perspectives and their corresponding impacts on the educational outcomes in their African colonies. The British promoted economic expansion underscored by indirect rule, that is, a minimal degree of direct political interference, reflecting the principle that development within the colonial territories should be the direct responsibility of these territories. The French on the other hand, stressed direct political association of their territories to French rule. The consequences of these different systems of colonial engagement emerged in the postcolonial period detailing a much higher number of schools in the former British colonies than in the former French colonies. However, both systems were similar in the utilisation of local resources for the ultimate benefit of the respective colonial powers.

The issue of education remains one of the most difficult challenges that have faced African leaders since gaining independence. This challenge was passionately expressed in Nkrumah's inaugural speech at the opening of the newly established Institute of African Studies in Ghana:

> What sort of Institute of African Studies does Ghana want and have need of? In what way can Ghana make its own specific contribution to the advancement of knowledge about the peoples and cultures of Africa through past history and through contemporary problems? For what kind of service are we preparing students of this Institute and of our Universities? Are we sure that we have established here the best possible relationship between teachers and students? To what extent are our universities identified with the aspirations of Ghana and Africa? You who are working in this Institute — as research workers and assistants, teachers and students have a special responsibility for helping to answer these questions. I do, however, wish to take this opportunity to put to you some of the guiding principles which an Institute of African Studies situated here in Ghana at this period of our history must constantly bear in mind. First and foremost, I would emphasise the need for a re-interpretation and a new assessment of the factors which make up our past. We have to recognise frankly that African studies, in the form in which they have been developed in the universities and centres of learning in the West, have been largely influenced by the concepts of old style "colonial studies,"

and still to some extent, remain under the shadow of colonial ideologies and mentality.

Until recently, the study of African history was regarded as a minor and marginal theme within the framework of imperial history. The study of African social institutions and cultures was subordinated in varying degrees to the effort to maintain the apparatus of colonial power. In British Institutes of higher learning, for example, there was a tendency to look to social anthropologists to provide the kind of knowledge that would help to support the particular brand of colonial policy known as indirect rule.

The study of African languages was closely related to the practical objectives of the European missionary and the administrator. African music, dancing and sculpture were labelled "primitive art." They were studied in such a way as to reinforce the picture of African society as something grotesque, as a curious, mysterious human backwater, which helped to retard social progress in Africa and to prolong colonial domination over its peoples.

African economic problems, organisation, labour, immigration, agriculture, communications, industrial development were generally viewed from the standpoint of the European interest in the exploitation of African resources, just as African politics were studied in the context of the European interest in the management or manipulation of African affairs.

When I speak of a new interpretation and new assessment, I refer particularly to our Professors and Lecturers. The non-Ghanaian non-African Professors and Lecturers are, of course, welcome to work here with us. Intellectually, there is no barrier between us and them. We appreciate, however, that their mental make-up has been largely influenced by their system of education and the facts of their society and environment. For this reason, they must endeavour to adjust and re-orientate their attitudes and thought to our African conditions and aspirations. They must not try simply to reproduce here their own diverse patterns of education and culture. They must embrace and develop those aspirations and responsibilities which are clearly essential for maintaining a progressive and dynamic African society.

One essential function of this Institute must surely be to study the history, culture and institutions, languages and arts of Ghana and of Africa in new African-centred ways — in entire freedom from the propositions and pre-suppositions of the colonial epoch, and from the distortions of those Professors and Lecturers who continue to make European studies of Africa the basis of this new assessment. By the work of this Institute, we must re-assess and assert the glories and achievements of our African past and inspire our generation, and succeeding generations, with a vision of a better future.

Nkrumah went further to include the study of Africans in the diaspora:

But you should not stop here. Your work must also include a study of the origins and culture of peoples of African descent in the Americas and the Caribbean, and you should seek to maintain close relations with their scholars so that there may be cross fertilisation between Africa and those who have their roots in the African past[56].

Over half a century since Nkrumah's speech Ghana and the rest of Africa continue to struggle for an appropriate and effective system of education that can help to lift Africans from poverty to better future prospects. Although progress has been made, for example, in the provision of education for a larger number of Africans than during the colonial years nonetheless the state of education in the African world continues to face formidable obstacles. In addition to the insufficient focus on science and technology education, lack of resources to strongly support the quality of the educational direction and experience raises much concern for the future.

---

[56] See http://nkrumahinfobank.org/article.php?id=440&c=51

Future Education

What kind of education is relevant in sustaining a better future for the African world? While the tragic consequences of the bitter legacy of Africans gathered through the ages persist, it is from this same source that a new hope for a better world can evolve. In other words, the destruction of Africa's past through conquests, if properly understood and harnessed by current and future generations of Africans can provide the basis for the renaissance of Africa and the world, in short, the endowment of an opportunity for a new beginning.

The dominant educational models in Africa have followed trajectories that have so far not been fully effective in aiding Africans to successfully engage with useful solutions to some of their pressing problems. For the future, some changes will be required to take root, for an effective African education. A change for instance, from stifling learning conditions where students are merely expected to be passive learners to an educational experience that places the emphasis on raising questions and challenging established norms for clearer understanding cannot be overstated. Such a focus will naturally require the materialisation of supportive learning conditions that encourage and promote creative thinking and problem solving in order to demonstrate their pertinent connections to African issues in particular, and those of the world in general. A broad knowledge and understanding of the African past must be an essential part of such a future education in order to provide the proper context for the appreciation of the multifaceted and difficult problems facing Africans. It is through the understanding of the past and its impact on the present that Africans can nurture the clarity of purpose to strengthen the development of durable solutions to problems facing Africans struggling for a better future.

Without science and technology it is difficult to envisage constructive progress in Africa, a case that is not lost on Africans, but what they desperately need is the total commitment to raise the importance and urgency of achieving the goal of promoting science and technology to the highest level in the educational process and beyond. A commitment to promoting science and technology will require substantial long-term resources.

From the onset of decolonisation African leaders have unceasingly acknowledged the criticality of education for genuine development but unfortunately beyond the rhetoric much is yet to be done to show their commitment to making education central to African development and progress. Considering the fact that there can be no real educational revolution without a well-organised and clear approach towards achieving reasonably effective results suggests that the difficult task of doing so successfully could be approached in phases. Thankfully, such phases already exist as presented within the arrangement of basic, secondary and tertiary levels of education, so the challenge going forward hinges on the planning, delivery and effective management of these phases.

One phase that appears to not enjoy a targeted focus as centred on the three mentioned earlier is apprenticeship. In spite of its criticality in human civilisation, the complex nature of apprenticeship can give it a misleading bearing within the notion of education as it can begin formally or informally at any phase of the educational process. As a form of learning that is purposefully focused on the development of practical proficiencies in a craft or trade, apprenticeship remains to be given the importance it requires to play its role in the development of the vital skills needed for development across Africa. The systematic targeting of apprenticeship towards a craft or trade must be made not only a key element in the development plans of African governments but above all actively given the support needed to elevate it to its deserved standing. A United Nations[57] report noted that technical and vocational education and training (TVET) in Africa is a challenge for all African states. It noted that the enrolment rate in formal TVET at secondary education phase is below 5% in most African states. In Africa non-formal and therefore non-certificated apprenticeship is predominant and often fragmented as learning opportunities that occur at the workplace in various capacities and initiatives promoted under non-educational auspices are inclined to operate in a non-coherent manner. The report notes that the potential demand for apprenticeship is huge as three out of five unemployed in sub-Saharan Africa are young people surviving mostly in the informal economic sector. However, in spite of the rising need for training across Africa, only a few African governments are able to finance quality apprenticeship training.

Clearly, without a concerted effort as already indicated Africa is likely to face a future with a growing unskilled population of unemployable youth. The absurdity of the situation is that notwithstanding the need for a competently skilled workforce to deliver development in Africa a negative social bias persists towards apprenticeship in Africa (Kitainge, 2004; Amedome &

---

[57] See http://www.unesco.org/new/en/dakar/education/technical-and-vocational-education-and-training/

Fiagbe, 2013; Kemevor & Kassah, 2015). Commenting of the models of apprenticeship from a German-European perspective, Greinert (2010) presents a relevant perspective:

> Concepts and institutions of a 'pedagogy of qualification for employment' are not coincidental constructs in the sense of providing unlimited quantities of technological arrangements, but are strongly embedded in structures of typical national cultures of work. In order to gain a first overview, one can proceed from the assumption that comprehensive system structures exist, which have emerged in their respective countries over a more or less long period of time. Systems or models of qualification for employment are social systems of action (p252).

What kinds of cultures of work now exist in Africa? How favourable are they to appreciating and promoting training for apprentices across the vocational spectrum? Answers to these questions are important for reconsidering the role of such training in Africa's development. In anticipation of the importance of education and training for the emancipation of African Americans, Hubert Harrison (1997), a civil rights intellectual writing in 1920, had the following to say:

> For in this work-a-day world people ask first, not "Where were you educated?" but "What do you know?" and next, "What can you do with it?" And if we of the Negro race can master modern knowledge – the one that counts – we will be able to win for our selves the priceless gifts of freedom and power, and we will be able to hold them against the world (p128).

The point about the importance of education in the context of African development and regeneration cannot be exaggerated. But can the current conventional model effectively serve the needs of the Africa people? What can we deduce from the results of the conventional models of education employed in Africa over the last fifty years? Adequate time has now elapsed leaving clear evidence for Africans to judge the overall efficacy of the systems of education that they have followed.

The unique historical experiences of the African people will require a unique model based on openness to new ideas and the re-examination of dormant African epistemologies (Nyamnjoh, 2011). In order to properly and honestly chart a reasonable path to unlocking the restrained talents of Africans a sustained commitment will be required to bring such a project to fruition, and only those willing to provide exceptional leadership are likely to obtain any measure of success.

A new beginning is crying out to be born, one that is based on a higher level of moral standing that current educational systems are finding challenging to reach. It is arguable that the current educational models that have dominated the world over the recent centuries to which Africa is also tethered have certain limitations in spite of their universal acceptability in providing the specific support needed by Africans in making education relevant to their circumstances.

Illich (2004) presented a forceful argument highlighting the ineffectual nature of institutionalised education:

> Universal education through schooling is not feasible. It would be no more feasible if it were attempted by means of alternative institutions built on the style of present schools. Neither new attitudes of teachers toward their pupils nor the proliferation of educational hardware or software (in classroom or bedroom), nor finally the attempt to expand the pedagogue's responsibility until it engulfs his pupils' lifetimes will deliver universal education. The current search for new educational *funnels* must be reversed into the search for their institutional inverse: educational webs

which heighten the opportunity for each one to transform each moment of his living into one of learning, sharing, and caring (p.vii).

Illich went on to say:

> Many students, especially those who are poor, intuitively know what the schools do for them. They school them to confuse process and substance. Once these become blurred, a new logic is assumed: the more treatment there is, the better are the results; or, escalation leads to success. The pupil is thereby "schooled" to confuse teaching with learning, grade advancement with education, a diploma with competence, and fluency with the ability to say something new. His imagination is "schooled" to accept service in place of value (p1)

The tragic consequence for the African tied to the educational conditions Illich attempted to articulate is that the inherent nature of such an educational system inevitably produces winners and losers instead of caring human beings, a system founded mostly on educational content that has essentially rendered the African a loser. A fitting expression in the spirit of Bell's (1992) observation captures the mood that the magical faces at the bottom of the well of universal educational system belong to the Africans.

At this early stage of the twenty-first century we face a future potentially charged with profound fundamental changes that only those who commit to preparedness stand to become its heirs. Africans have made the journey, torturous as it may have been, to this unique point in human history is a testament to their tenacity to survive and hope for a more soothing future. Such a future is within their reach, deliverable through an educational system unique to their circumstances. One that will require foresight, commitment, courage and above all the desire to offer a model equipped to restore compassion in an increasingly detached technological future world.

CONCLUSION

No one knows the future. Yet consciously or not we constantly make plans for the future. Having some clarity may be advantageous when peering into the future. There is nowhere on earth far more complex than Africa, in terms of its role as the cradle of human development and propagation across the world, the diversity of its people, their historical developments and political experiences. The depth of complexity that constitutes Africa must be appreciated for any meaningful projection of the future for Africa. In our attempt to imagine the African future we first directed our attention to surveying the major development that occurred predominantly in the last century in order to form a basis for a reasonable discussion of the future for Africans.

We considered the political struggles that characterised the African experience throughout the last century, focusing on a number of important African states that emerged from the struggles to end colonialism. Our discussions of these states also did not preclude descendent of Africans in the Diaspora as it is reasonable to give due recognition to the descendants of Africans in recent history who were forcibly removed from the African continent. The states discussed revealed their numerous economic and political problems since gaining independence and their relationship with both the Western and Eastern nations were examined to provide a setting to inform some of the possible future directions open to Africans.

We observed that gaining freedom ultimately shifted the responsibility entirely to Africans for determining their future choices. What lies beyond freedom must necessarily include among others the commitment to responsibility and self-sacrifice, and for any measure of success in the context of African wellbeing will require understanding, vision and unconditional commitment from African leaders to create the most favourable conditions for the best future outcomes for Africans. Over half a century of African self-determination has outlined the difficulties that remain to be fully tackled and defeated. Issues regarding the promotion of democratic facilities and the handling of political power, social opportunities that the people can enjoy through health improvement and human resource maximisation must all be given the genuine attention they deserve for genuine solutions. Furthermore, the intractable issues with future climatic changes, the environment and the challenges of sustainable living will all require credible responses. These challenges, as we observed, offer unique opportunities in galvanising the resolve of Africans to utilise their diversity as a major source of strength to shape a new understanding and cooperation toward tackling the problems currently facing Africa, and using the experiences gathered as the basis for preparing for an unknown future, one that is very likely to present, among many other unknowns, inter-state issues.

Africa is indeed at the crossroads (Williams, 1987; 2004) and must decide which way to go in our dynamic and increasingly confusing world. The choices facing

Africa at this historic point and the decisions to be taken rest solely with Africans, a responsibility that they cannot avoid and must fully accept. Critical factors in taking any beneficial decisions for Africa will require leadership that demonstrates responsibility and commitment to care for the African people, and the vision to chart the most productive route for African survival and renewal.

The problem of the twenty-first century for Africa, as noted by John Henrik Clarke, is the regaining and controlling of power. A point echoed by Harrison (1997) in his view of the rewards of education for the African world. While it is important for Africa to overcome the key disadvantages that it faces through regaining its power, the challenge in controlling such power is immense. The African leadership that will come must guard against the malevolent trait of power noted by Russell (2004):

> The success of insanity, in literature, in philosophy, and in politics, is one of the peculiarities of our age, and the successful form of insanity proceeds almost entirely from impulses towards power (p269).

The African world has endured much suffering through the ages as a consequence of the misuse of power by the forces to which it fell victim. And if all conditions continue to remain the same into the foreseeable future then obviously negligible relief will be the outcome for the African world. However, we have discussed some of the factors critical to bringing some productive future prospects to the present debilitating condition of the African world.

What should be the guiding principle for an African world that sets itself up ready for restoration? It should be highly conscious of the powerful moral position that it has been afforded as a result of the anguish endured over centuries. Leaders such as Martin Luther King and Nelson Mandela provide examples of the humanity that should underpin the mentality of the new African world. Such an outlook will necessarily require courage, perseverance, commitment to justice and an inclusive vision for a harmonious world as examples among other desirable elements. Thus an African world ready for renewal would have a critical mass of Africans and people of recent African descent conscious of their ancient heritage and quietly confident about their purpose in the creation of a better future for the world. Their confidence will be informed by their knowledge and understanding of the African experience in the context of our present age and its importance in the positive transformation of humanity.

An African world ready for renewal would initiate a system of education that will aim to build the confidence of the African by raising the awareness of the African contribution to world development from antiquity to our present age and the possibility of generating new positive perspectives for the future. In such a system the focus would be on the development of the full potentialities of the individual as an essential process in providing each with the appropriate resources for meeting the complexities of the African situation. As a result of focusing on the individual it would be organized to resist the signs of an industrial scale process by which the quality of the experience is sacrificed for mediocrity. It would be programmed to challenge individuals to rise to the highest levels of their productive abilities, and once developed to use those abilities for the greater good of Africa and for the promotion of compassion and fairness in the world.

An African world ready for renewal would have unity and justice as the basis for its political life. The guiding constitution and the laws that flow from it are applied in fairness to all concerned. It would be truly representative of the people, making it possible for their wishes to be fully expressed, acknowledged and studied for implementation. It would acknowledge differences in terms of talents and harness them for the benefit of all. Its system of dissemination of information does not seek to mould or distort the truth but to reflect public opinion. The leaders in its political life would be individuals without personal ambitions beyond that of the highest service and without a desire for wealth or power to be gained in serving the people.

An African world ready for renewal would have compassion and cooperation as the standard for its economic interpretation of existence. It would seek to eliminate poverty through cooperation where every individual is a valued participant in the production of wealth and wellbeing. It would seek to make the improvement of the human being the dominating motive rather than the making of profit through the exploitation and degradation of the less fortunate. At its core will be the desire to use its economic system to contribute to the lifting of humanity to a new higher understanding of human existence.

For the hopeful, the future is always filled with great possibilities. On the other hand, without hope life itself becomes pointless to preserve for any future possibilities. But one can only be hopeful when one is imbued with a sense of confidence and vision to act on present circumstances for the desired future outcomes. Africans have proved their resilience as they continue to remain hopeful in spite of all the heavy blows that events through the ages have seriously and mercilessly dealt them. While the African hardiness may engender admiration they cannot drift along to their possible future and final annihilation just hoping but should act forcefully for favourable positive future changes. In our present world where man has abundantly demonstrated his capacity for destruction as a result of the needless defective relationship amongst men, the potential for Africans to play a leading role in the creation of a harmonious future world is imaginable.

REFERENCES

Achebe, C. The Trouble with Nigeria. England: Heinemann, 1984.

Addo, K.A. and B. Amisigo & P.K. Ofori-Danson L.L. Larbi. "Impacts of Coastal Inundation Due to Climate Change in a CLUSTER of Urban Coastal Communities in Ghana, West Africa." 7 September 2011. Remote Sensing. 7 April 2015 <http://www.mdpi.com>.

Alden, C. China in Africa. London: Zed Books, 2009.

Amanor, K.S. "Global resource grabs, agribusiness concerntration and the smallholder: two West African case studies." Journal of Peasant Studies (2012): 739 - 749.

Amedome, S.K & Fiagbe, Y.A.K. "Challenges Facing Technical And Vocational Education in Ghana." International Journal of Scientific & Technology Research 2.6 (2013): 253-255.

Anderson, C. Powernomics. Bethesda: Powernomics Coporation of America, 2001.

Ayittey, G.B.N. Africa Unchained. New York, 2006.

Baird, V. "Toal Control." New Internationalist 1 April 2015: 12-16.

Barnett, T. & Whiteside, A. AIDS in the Twenty-First Century. Hampshire: Palgrave, 2006.

Bartels, F.L. "Philip Quaque 1741 - 1816." Transactions of the Gold Coast & Togoland Historical Society 1.5 (1955): 153-177.

Bassett-Jones, N. "The Paradox of Diversity Management, Creativity and Innovation." Diversity

Management, Creativity and Innovation 14.2 (2005): 169 - 175.

Bayart, J.F. The State in Africa. Cambridge: Polity Press, 2014.

Bell, D. Faces at the Bottom of the Well. New York, 1992.

Bennett, L. The Shaping of Black America. New York: Penguin Books, 1993.

Berkeley, B. The Graves Are Not Yet Full. New York: Basic Books, 2001.

Boateng, F. "African Traditional Education: A Method of Disseminating Cultural Values." Journal of Black Studies 13 (1983): 321-336.

Boko, M., I. Niang, A. Nyong, C. Vogel, A. Githeko, M. Medany, B. Osman-Elasha, R. Tabo and P. YandaBoko, M., I. Niang, A. Nyong, C. Vogel, A. Githeko, M. Medany, B. Osman-Elasha, R. Tabo and Yanda, P. Africa: Climate Change 2007: Impacts, Adaptation and Vulnerability. Contribution of Working Group 11 to the Fourth Assessment Report of the Intergovernmental Panel on Climate Change. Cambridge: Cambridge University Press, 2007.

Booth, J. Africa for the African. Zomba: Kachere Series, 1897/2007.

Césaire, A. Discourse on Colonialism. New York: Monthly Review Press, 2000.

Chan, S. The Morality of China in Africa. London: Zed Books, 2013.

Conway, G. The science of climate change in Africa: impacts and adaptation. London: Imperial College, 2009.

Cotula, L. The great African land grab? London: Zed Books, 2013.

Dams, World Commission on. Dams and Development. Kent: Earthscan Publications Ltd, 2000.

Davidson, B. Which Way Africa . Middlesex: Penguin Books, 1964.

Deane, P.D. The first Industrial Revolution. Cambridge: Cambridge University Press, 1965.

deGraft-Johnson, J.C. "African Traditional Education." Presence Africaiane (1956): 51-55.

Dennis, B. Slaves to Racism: An Unbroken Chain From America to Liberia. New York: Agora Publishing, 2008.

Diop, C.A. Black Africa. Westport: Lawrence Hill & Company, 1978.

Dubois, W.E.B. Souls of Black Folk. New York: Penguin Books, 1996.

DuBois, W.E.B. The Negro Problem - The Talented Tenth. New York: James Pott & Company, 1903.

Economic Intelligenece Unit. The future of healthcare in Africa. London: The Economist, 2011.

Ehrhart, H. LeGoff, M. Rocher, E. Singh, R.J. Does Migration Foster Exports? Evidence from Africa. Washington: The World Bank, 2014.

Ekeh, P.P. "Social Anthropology and Two Contrasting Uses of Tribalism in Africa." Comparative Studies in Society and History 32.4 (1990): 660 - 700.

Fanon, F. Black Skinn, White Mask. London: Pluto Press, 1993.

Feinstein, A. The Shadow World. London: Penguin Books, 2011.

Fenby, J. History of Modern China. London: Penguin Books, 2013.

Fetter, B. "The Union Miniere and Its Hinterland: A Demographic Reconstruction." African Economic History: Business Empires in Equitorial Africa 12 (1983): 67 - 81 .

Fraser, A.G. "Native Education in Africa." Journal of the Royal Society of Arts 81.4208 (1933): 813 - 831.

Garnier, M. and M. Schafer. "Educational Model and Expansion of Enrollments in Sub-Saharan Africa." Sociology of Education 79.2 (2006): 153-175.

Gough, S. & Scott, W. "Education and sustainable development: a political analysis." Education Review (2003).

Greinert, W. "Governance Models of Training for Employment: a European perspective." Research in Comparative and International Education 5.3 (2010): 251-260.

Guevara, E. The African Dream. The Harvill Press, 2001.

Guggisberg, F.G. "The Goal of the Gold Coast." Journal of the Royal African Society 21.82 (1922): 81- 91.

Hamel, C.E. Black Morocco: A History of Slavery, Race and Islam. New York: Cambridge University Press, 2013.

Harrison, H.H. When Africa Awakes. Baltimore: Black Classic Press, 1997.

—. When Africa Awakes. Baltimore: Black Classic Press, 1997.

Hitti, P.K. History of the Arabs. Hampshire: Palgrave Macmillan, 2002.

Hochschild, A. King Leopold's Ghost. London: Pan Books, 2006.

Hourani, A. History of the Arab Peoples. London: Faber & Faber, 2013.

Igue, J.O. "A New Generation of Leaders in Africa: What Issues do they Face?" International Development Policy (2010): 115 - 133 .

Iliffe, J. A Modern History of Tangantika. Cambridge: Cambridge University Press, 1994.

Illich, I. Deschooling Society. London: Marion Boyars Publishers Ltd, 2004.

Jervan, M. Poor Numbers. New York: Cornell University Press, 2013.

Johnson, L. & Dorrington, R. The Impact of AIDS on Orphanhood in South Africa: A Quantitative Analysis. Cape Town: Univ of Cape Town: Centre for Actural Research, 2001.

Katzenellengogen, S. E. "The miner's frontier, transport and general economic development." Gann, L H and P Duignan. Colonialism in Africa, 1870-1960. The economics of colonialism. Cambridge: Cambridge University Press, 1975. 360-426.

Keay, J. China: A History. London: Harper Press, 2009.

Keita, L. "Philosophy and Development: On the Problematic African Development - A Diachronic Analysis." Keita, L. Philosophy and African Development. Daker: Council for the Development of Social Science Research in Africa, 2011. 115-137.

Kemevor, A.K. & Kassah, J.K. "Challenges of Technical and Vocational Education and Training and Educational Stakeholders in the Volta Region of Ghana ." International Journal of Humanities Social Sciences and Education 2.6 (2015): 70-79.

Kitainge, K.M. "Reforming education and training? Lessons from development of vocational education and training in Kenya." Austraian Journal of Adult Learning 44.1 (2004): 44-61.

Kodjo, E. Africa Today. Accra: Ghana Universities Press, 1989.

Lindqvist, S. Exterminate All the Brutes. London: Granta Books, 2002.

Lindsay, S.W. & Martens, W.J.M. Maleria in the African highlands: past, present and future. Geneva: World Health Organisation, 1998.

Maathai, W. The Challenge for Africa. London: Arrow Books, 2010.

Mahajan, V. Africa Rising: How 900 Million African Consumers Offer More Than You Think. New Jersey: Prentice Hall, 2009.

Mazrui, A.A. "Black Africa and the Arabs." Foreign Affairs 53.4 (1975): 725 - 742.

McLeod, P.L. Lobel, S.A. Cox, T.H. "Ethnic Diversity and Creativity in Small Groups." Small Group Research 27.2 (1996): 248 - 264.

Memmi, A. Cassirer, T. Twomeysource, M.G. "The Impossible life of Franz Fanon." The Massachusetts Review 14.1 (1973): 9 - 39.

Memmi, A. The colonizer and the colonized. Oxon: Earthscan, 2003.

Meyers, A.R. "Class, Ethnicity, and Slavery: The Origins of the Moroccan Abid." The International Journal of African Historical Studies 10.3 (1977): 427 - 442.

Morella, E. Foster, V. Banerjee, S.G. Climbing the Ladder: The State of Snitation in Sub-Saharan Africa. Washington: The world Bank, 2008.

Moyo, D. Winner Takes All. London: Penguin Books, 2012.

Mumford, W.B. "Malangali School." Africa: Journal of the International African Institute 3.3 (1930): 269 - 292.

Nkidumana, L. & Boyce, J.K. Africa's Odious Debts. London: Zed Books, 2011.

Nkrumah, K. Challenge of the Congo. London: Panaf Books, 2002.

—. Dark days in Ghana. London: Panaf Books, 2001.

—. Ghana: The Autobiography of Kwame Nkrumah. New York: International Publishers, 1957.

—. Neo-colonialism, the last stage of imperialism. London: Panaf Books, 2004.

Nyamnjoh, F.B. "A Relevant Education for African Develoment." Keita, L. Philosophy and African Development. Daker: Council for the Development of Social Science Research in Africa, 2011. 139-154.

Nye, J.S. The Future of Power. New York: Public Affairs, 2011.

Okoth-Owiro, A. The Nile Treaty: State Succession and International Treaty Commitments: A case Study of the

Nile Water Treaties. Nairobi: Konrad Adenauer Foundation, 2004.

Omari, T.P. Kwame Nkrumah: The Anatomy of an African Dictator. Accra: Sankofa Educational Publishers, 1970.

Omolewa, M. "Traditional African Modes of Education: Their Relevance in the Modern World." International Review of Education (2007): 593-612.

Orr, D.W. Ecological Literacy: Education and the Transition to a Postmodern World. New York: State University of New York, 1992.

Phillips, K.W. "How Diversity Makes Us Smarter." Scientific American 311.4 (2014).

Phillipson, R.H.L. Linguistic Imperialism. Oxford: Oxford University Press, 1992.

Pillay, P. Access to essential services: Education and Health. Sizanang: HumanResource Research Council, 2005.

Postma, D.W. "Taking the Future Seriously: On t he inadequacies of the Framework of Liberalism for Environmental Education." Journal of Philosophy of Education 36.1 (2002): 41 - 56.

Rees, M. Our Final Century. London: William Heinemann, 2003.

Roberstson, C. The Fastest Billion: The Story Behind Africa's Economic Revolution. London: Renaissance Capital, 2012.

Rodney, W. How Europe Underdeveloped Africa. London: Bogel-L'ouverture, 1988.

Russell, B. Power. Abingdon: Routledge, 2004.

Sbacchi, A. Legacy of Bitterness: Ethiopia and Facist Italy, 1935-41. New Jersey: The Red Sea Press, Inc., 1997.

Sen, A. Development as Freedom. New York: Anchor Books, 2000.

Shaxson, A. Poison Wells. Hampshire: Palgrave Macmillan, 2008.

Siegfried, W.R. "Preservation of species in southern African nature reserves." Huntley, B. Biotic Diversity in Southern Africa: Concepts and Conservation. Cape Town: Oxford University Press, 1989.

Sithole, A. "Ghana: A Beacon of Hope in Africa." Policy and Practice Brief 018 (2012): 1-9.

Smith, D. The State of the World Atlas. Oxford: New Internationalist, 2013.

Sultan, B. Guan, K. Kouressy, M. Piani, C. Hammer, G.L **McLean**, G. & Lobell, D.B. "Robust features of future climate change impacts on sorghum yields in West Africa." Environ. Res. Lett. 9 (2014).

Tanner, A. Emigration, Brain Drain and Development. Helsinki: East-West Books, 2005.

Tedla, E. "Indigenous african Education as a Means for Understanding The Fullness of Life: Amara Traditional Education." Journal of Black Studies 23.1 (1992): 7-26.

The World Bank. Can Africa Claim the 21st Century? Washington: The World Bank, 2000.

The World Commission on Environment and Developmemt. Our Common Future. Oxford: Oxford university Press, 2009.

Thomas, C.D. "Extinction risk from climate change." Nature (2004): 145 - 148.

Tibedu, T. The Making of Modern Ethiopia 1896-1974. New Jersey: The Red Sea Press, Inc., 1995.

Toffolo, C.E. The Arab League. Chelsea: Chelsea House, 2008.

UN. World AIDS Day Report. Geneva: UNAIDS, 2012.

van Wyk, J.A. "The African union response to climate change and climate security." Mwiturubani, D.A. & van Wyk, J.A. Climate change and natural resources conflict in Africa. Institute for Sercurity Studies, 2010.

vanderPloeg, A.J. "Education in Colonial Africa: The German Experience." Comparative Education Review (1977): 91-109.

Washington, B.T. Up From Slavery. New York: Penguin Books, 1986.

Wells, S. The Journey of Man. London: Penguin Books, 2003.

White, B.W. "Talk about School: Educational and the Colonial Project in French and British Africa. (1860 - 1960)." Comparative Education (1996): 9 - 25.

Williams, C. The Distruction of Black Civilization. Chicago: Third Wordl Press, 1987.

—. The Rebirth of African Civilization. Chicago: Third World Press, 2004.

World Economic and Financial Surveys. Regional Economic Outlook: Sub-Saharan Africa Fostering Durable and Inclusive Growth. Washington: Internation Monetary Fund, 2014.

—. Regional Economic Outlook: Sub-Saharan Africa Sustaining the Expansion. Washington: International Monetaary Fund, 2011.

INDEX

D

E

F